BANK

GW00374245

Hope this cures
your insomnia)

[signature]

BANKING

An introductory text

PHILIP MOLYNEUX

MACMILLAN

First published 1990 by
MACMILLAN PRESS LTD
Houndmills, Basingstoke, Hampshire RG21 6XS
and London
Companies and representatives
throughout the world

ISBN 0–333–54119–7 hardcover
ISBN 0–333–54120–2 paperback

A catalogue record for this book is available
from the British Library.

10   9   8   7   6   5   4   3
04   03   02   01   00   99   98   97   96

Printed in Hong Kong

CONTENTS

v

LIST OF FIGURES

LIST OF TABLES

PREFACE

Banking markets have witnessed considerable change over the last decade and the pace of change will no doubt continue given 1992 and the inevitability of a single European banking market. The aim of the text is to provide a detailed coverage of the UK banking and financial system together with an overview of various theoretical issues relating to banking. In addition this text analyses the main trends and developments affecting UK and European banks. The first half of the book concentrates on the UK financial system and various theoretical issues whereas the second part places greater emphasis on various international aspects, especially the implications of 1992. In particular, Chapter 8 examines the main regulatory issues facing UK and European banks, Chapter 9 covers recent trends and developments in banking, Chapter 10 looks at money markets and international banking and the final chapter examines in detail the main characteristics of European Community banking markets.

The bulk of this book is based on my first-year undergraduate lecture notes for banking and finance students at the University College of North Wales, Bangor. Many thanks to Helen Treece for doing an effective job on a difficult manuscript and to the staff of the Institute of European Finance for the time and resources they afforded on work relating to this text. Finally, I wish to thank Delyth, Lois and Rhiannon, without whose encouragement and understanding this text would never have been completed.

PHILIP MOLYNEUX

ACKNOWLEDGEMENTS

The author and publishers are grateful to the University of London External Advisory Service for copyright permission to reproduce some of the author's lecture notes that have appeared in a different form in their *BSc (Economics) Degree Banking One Study Guide*; and to the editors of *Regional Studies* for use of part of an article that appeared in the December 1989 issue (used in the final chapter of this text).

.

CHAPTER 1

GENERAL DESCRIPTION OF THE UK FINANCIAL SYSTEM

INSTITUTIONAL STRUCTURE

The UK financial system is characterised by a broad institutional coverage and, in many sectors, a strong international orientation. Prior to the growth in eurobanking business and the proliferation of secondary banks during the 1960s and 1970s, traditional banking business was dominated by the main London clearing banks (LCBs). The picture has changed significantly since that time. In the mid-1950s the main clearers accounted for over two-thirds of total bank sterling deposit liabilities compared with just over one-half in December 1989. Table 1.1 shows that the UK banks' share of total banking sector assets fell between December 1979 and December 1989.

Another interesting feature since 1979 is that there has been a substantial decline in the importance of US banks and a corresponding increase in the share of business undertaken by Japanese banks. This, coupled with recent capital market developments (Big Bang), as well as various deregulatory pressures, helps to illustrate the contemporary dynamic nature of the UK financial system.

Prior to the implementation of the Banking Act 1979 the UK banking sector had comprised institutions included on the statistical list of the Bank of England. This included banks, discount houses and the Banking Department of the Bank of England. Inclusion on the statistical list, which existed for many years, was based chiefly on informal appraisal of a bank's size and reputation and was usually closely associated with the granting of authorised bank status for exchange control purposes. The Banking Act 1979 required the Bank of England to publish lists of recognised banks and licensed deposit takers, of which some of the former and many

1

of the latter were not included on the old statistical list. Together with the abolition of exchange controls in 1979, this rendered the old banking sector definition inappropriate. The new extended sector, known as the monetary sector, came into effect from the end of December 1981, and it comprised:

1. all recognised banks and licensed deposit takers,
2. institutions listed in the Channel Islands and the Isle of Man that comply with UK monetary control arrangements,
3. the Trustee Savings Banks,
4. Girobank
5. The Banking Department of the Bank of England.

A general description of the system encompasses an overview of the main types of financial institutions operating in the market, and these can be classified as follows:

1. reporting banks,
2. other deposit-taking institutions,
3. other financial intermediaries.

DEPOSIT-TAKING INSTITUTIONS

Reporting banks

This group receives its name from the fact that it consists of all banks that report monthly to the Bank of England. It includes the retail (clearing) banks, accepting houses, other British banks and other foreign banks. At the beginning of 1988, 258 UK and 373 foreign bank branches and subsidiaries reported on a monthly basis to the Bank of England. By far the most important domestic group are the retail banks, which accounted for 56.8 per cent of total sterling deposits and 31.7 per cent of total banking sector assets at the end of 1989; technically, the 'banking sector' in this section refers to the new monetary sector excluding the discount houses. The retail banks have been known traditionally as the clearing banks because they deal with the majority of the country's cheque and credit clearing.

Table 1.1 *Reporting Banks' Total Assets and Sterling Deposits, December 1979 and December 1989*

	£ million		Percentages	
	Dec. 1979	Dec. 1989	Dec. 1979	Dec. 1989
Total assets				
Retail (clearing) banks	62,198	391,702	23.6	31.7
Accepting houses	10,251	51,535	3.9	4.2
Other UK banks	39,025	61,039	14.8	4.9
Total	111,474	504,276	42.3	40.8
American banks	59,228	118,697	22.4	9.6
Japanese banks	29,165	281,992	11.1	22.8
Other overseas banks	53,329	329,268	20.2	26.7
Consortium banks	10,648	—	4.1	—
Total	152,370	729,957	57.7	59.1
Overall total	263,841	1,234,233	100.0	100.0
Sterling deposits				
Retail (clearing) banks	42,638	266,422	55.4	56.8
Accepting houses	3,858	28,916	5.0	6.2
Other UK banks	15,417	38,524	20.0	8.2
Total	61,913	333,862	80.4	71.2
American banks	7,438	17,338	9.7	3.7
Japanese banks	560	33,315	0.7	7.1
Other overseas banks	6,193	84,946	8.1	18.1
Consortium banks	810	—	1.1	—
Total	15,001	135,599	19.6	28.9
Overall total	76,914	469,461	100.0	100.0

Source: Bank of England Quarterly Bulletin (various issues)

Six London and Scottish clearing bank groups dominate this sector: Barclays, Lloyds, Midland, National Westminster, Royal Bank of Scotland and Bank of Scotland. The first four, the 'Big Four', have extensive branch networks throughout England and Wales, whereas the branch network of the other two is predominantly in Scotland. The London clearing banks (LCBs) accounted for approximately 60 per cent of sterling advances to UK residents in late 1989 compared with the Scottish clearing banks' 8 per cent. They also have much larger branch networks, 10 481, compared with 1785 for the Scottish clearers.

Girobank, the state-owned institution established in 1968 to offer money transmission services through post offices, as well as the Trustee Savings Bank (officially listed in September 1986) and the Co-operative Bank are also members of the centralised clearing system in London. (Girobank is to be sold to a building society in 1990 after an unsuccessful attempt at privatisation in late 1988.) Recent deregulation of the British payments systems, following the Child Report (1984) took effective responsibility away from the Committee of London and Scottish Bankers and vested it in a new body, APACS, the Association for Payment Clearing Services.

The 'Big Four' London clearing banks offer a wide range of banking products and services to the general public, and they dominate the money transmission facilities within the United Kingdom. Their subsidiary companies, many of which are themselves recognised banks or licensed deposit takers, concentrate on offering specialised services and facilities many with a bias towards the requirements of their parents' larger corporate domestic and overseas customers. Some foreign subsidiaries, however, provide a wide range of banking services through branch networks in the territories in which they operate akin to the operations of their parents in the United Kingdom. Clearing banks offer traditional current and deposit account facilities, and in recent years have introduced interest-bearing chequing accounts. The clearing banks also play a large role in the market for wholesale deposits. The majority of their funding comes from these two sources.

The LCBs also dominate the retail and corporate lending markets in the United Kingdom. Retail customers have access to overdraft and short-term unsecured lending. Since 1980 the banks have also made major inroads into the longer-term house mortgage finance market. Their portion of net lending in the mortgage market has increased from 5 per cent in 1980 to 27 per cent by 1988, compared with a decline from 79 per cent to 51 per cent for building societies over the same period. Corporate banking facilities have been traditionally provided through the banks' merchant banking subsidiaries. These subsidiaries allow the clearers to provide a broad range of services, including mergers and acquisitions (M&A) business, new issues, equity participation and other areas of corporate advice.

Up to three years ago commercial banks dominated the bank lending market. Merchant banks were considered to be the prima donnas of corporate finance, stockbrokers acted as agents for debt and equity investors, and jobbers had a monopoly on market making in securities. Since the liberalisation of the UK financial markets on 27 October 1986, the four big clearing banks have expanded their brokerage and securities business. Through their merchant banking arms, together with the purchasing of jobbing and broking firms, banks now undertake business ranging from equities market-making and primary dealing in gilts to more traditional lines of business.

The 16 accepting houses, all members of the Accepting Houses Committee, form the 'top echelon' of the merchant banking sector. These banks have a special relationship with the central banking authorities, and their sterling acceptances are eligible for rediscount at the Bank of England. In addition to acceptance credits these banks also provide a broad range of corporate finance and investment management services. They are heavily involved in the new issues of securities and mergers and acquisitions business. The accepting houses also have investment subsidiaries that manage mutual funds (unit trusts), investment trusts and large securities portfolios for private as well as institutional investors. Accepting houses and related companies provide a wide range of other services that include leasing, insurance broking, export finance, bullion dealing and the provision of venture capital.

There are many other merchant banks which perform the same functions as the accepting houses, but they do not have the same 'special' relationship with the Bank of England. The major non-accepting house merchant banks are subsidiaries of other banks (for example, County NatWest and Barclays de Zoete Wedd) as well as various British overseas banks.

The Bank of England classification (other British banks) is a 'catch-all' category, which 'comprises all other UK-registered institutions and certain institutions in the Channel Islands and the Isle of Man, which are either independent companies, or controlled by UK companies or by individuals'. By December 1987 there were 205 banks (including subsidiaries) in this group, ranging from British overseas banks, finance houses, trust companies, leasing firms and merchant banks to investment companies. Table 1.1 shows that these banks accounted for over 8 per cent of total banking sector sterling deposits in December 1989 and for 5.0 per cent of total banking sector assets.

At 31 December 1989 foreign banks held nearly 60 per cent of the UK banking system's total assets but only 28.9 per cent of total sterling deposits. There were approximately 370 (reporting) foreign-owned banks operating in London by late 1988, and they have tended to concentrate on commercial lending, trade finance and trading on the money markets. The US, Japanese and European banks are very active in the UK capital markets, and they offer a range of services similar to that of the UK merchant banks.

Many foreign banks purchased stockbrokers and jobbers prior to the reorganisation of the UK securities market on 27 October 1986. Typically the foreign banks have been involved primarily with wholesale and corporate banking services, although they do provide rather limited retail facilities. Some US institutions own finance house subsidiaries as well as small savings institutions. A noticeable feature in recent years has been the changing structure of the foreign bank sector, especially the growth in importance of the Japanese and the relative decline of the US banks. The former's percentage of total banking sector assets increased from 11.1 to 22.8 per cent between 1979 and 1989, whereas the corresponding figures for the US banks were 22.4 and 9.6 per cent respectively. Japanese banks' assets in the United Kingdom now exceed those of the clearing banks, and the bulk of their business is in non-sterling money market and corporate banking activities. Other overseas banks are dominated by European institutions and they are also an important sector.

Consortium banks are banks owned by other banks, in which no individual institution has a shareholding of more than 50 per cent, and in which at least one shareholder is based overseas. Consortium banks are mainly involved in the provision of foreign currency term lending, predominantly to overseas borrowers. These banks are also involved in syndicated loans and international bond issuing business. Since 1988 this category has been included in the other overseas banks statistics.

Other deposit-taking institutions

At the beginning of 1988 there were 138 building societies, with total assets exceeding £160,097 million, operating in the United Kingdom. In 1988 the building societies accounted for over 43 per cent of the total UK sterling deposits held by UK residents, compared with 38.2 per cent for the London and Scottish clearing banks. In fact, building societies have had a larger share of the market since 1975. Traditionally, this group has obtained funds from consumers through share and deposit balances, and used these mainly for financing home purchases. In terms of total deposits, the two largest UK building societies would rank amongst the world's largest 100 banks.

The 1986 Building Societies Act extended the traditional role of the building societies, and they are now able to offer a wider range of banking, investment, insurance and non-financial products. All the major building societies now offer chequing facilities, unsecured personal loans, insurance and securities broking services through their branch networks. In 1989 Abbey National had its shares listed on the London Stock Exchange and is now regarded as a bank offering a full range of banking services. Various government savings institutions also participate in the financial system. The National Savings Bank and Girobank offer their services through the Post Office. The National Savings Bank offers deposits and cash withdrawal facilities primarily for retail customers.

The eight discount house members of the London Discount Market Association, together with two firms of discount brokers and the money trading departments of five banks, comprise the London discount market. These institutions perform a unique function in the UK banking system. The main operation of the discount house is to discount and hold bills with funds borrowed at call from the banks; these bills can then be rediscounted with the banks or central bank. In general, the discount houses act as a buffer between the central bank and the banking system as a whole.

It is through the discount houses that the central bank operates as a lender of last resort. Most of the discount houses' funds are obtained through the short-term money markets, predominantly money at call and short notice from the banks. Funds borrowed by the discount houses are invested in a range of short-term assets.

OTHER INSTITUTIONS AND MARKETS

Non-bank financial intermediaries

Table 1.2 *Total Assets of the Major Non-bank Financial Intermediaries, December 1983 – December 1989 (£ million)*

	1983	1989
Building societies	87,190	188,683
Insurance and pension funds	225,520	425,099
Investment and unit trusts	26,799	67,132
Reporting banks	631,552	1,234,233

Sources: 1. Central Statistical Office, *Financial Statistics*, no. 252, March 1987 (adapted)
2. *Bank of England Quarterly Bulletins* (various issues)

Table 1.2 shows the total assets of the major non-bank financial intermediaries in the UK between 1983 and 1989. It can be seen that the insurance companies and pension funds are the second major group by asset size in the UK. Both hold the majority of their investments in company securities, long-term debt and property. They are the most important investing group in the UK capital market. Struthers and Speight (1986, p. 110) point out that by the beginning of 1985 insurance companies were:

the largest holders of UK government securities (around 30 per cent . . .) with the pension funds coming next (at around 16 per cent). In ordinary shares the pension funds are the largest holders with approximately 40 per cent of listed UK ordinary shares, . . . with the insurance companies next at around 18 per cent.

In the United Kingdom the domestic capital market has been dominated for a considerable time by institutional investors.

Because of their size and importance (dominance) as institutional investors, insurance companies and pension funds are likely to compete aggressively with other financial intermediaries in order to increase their market presence over the next decade.

UK financial markets

The International Stock Exchange of the United Kingdom and the Republic of Ireland (hereafter called the Stock Exchange for short) is the third largest exchange in the world and has floors in London and six provincial centres, one of which is Dublin. Traditionally, most of the business was carried out on the floor of the London exchange, but because of the rapid developments since Big Bang the Stock Exchange decided to close its trading floor on 2 March 1987. The decline of the trading floor began on 27 October 1986, when the Big Bang reforms were implemented. These included the introduction of new electronic price and trading information systems, which facilitated trading over the telephone and through various telecommunications links.

During 1986 the market for securities in the United Kingdom was considerably reorganised by new investor protection legislation, a dramatic change in the ownership and operations of the London exchange, and developments in the over-the-counter (OTC) market. A government investigation of Stock Exchange activities which began in 1983 (under the Restrictive Trade Practices Act of 1956) was called off when the Exchange agreed to abolish fixed commissions on securities transactions. In addition, traditional single capacity methods of trading, whereby only jobbers were allowed to buy and sell securities, were abolished. Single capacity, in which jobbing and brokerage business was clearly separated, was replaced by dual capacity.

From 27 October 1986 ('Big Bang' day), financial companies could undertake both broking and jobbing functions. Big Bang also ended restrictive practices in the gilts (government bonds) markets, where two jobbers previously dominated the markets. In late 1986 there were 27 firms listed as official primary dealers, making markets in gilts. In the run-up to the Big Bang the authorities allowed financial groups to acquire interests in British securities firms on the Stock Exchange, and they were permitted to take full control (100 per cent) of these firms on 1 March 1986. This led to a flood of purchases by both domestic and foreign banks. The market is now dominated by 33 leading players, including the largest American banks and Japanese securities houses. On 12 November 1986 the members of the Exchange voted in favour of reforms needed to clear the way for the merger of the Stock Exchange with the International Securities Regulatory Organisation (ISRO), which comprised 180 international securities houses in London. The two organisations are regulated by the Securities Association. This formed a new international market for the trading of shares and bonds, and enhanced London's position as a truly international financial centre.

For the majority of institutions operating in the market, their business is truly global, ranging from UK and international equities market-making, through the whole gamut of investment banking products right down to traditional retail banking business. Fewer than 20 large British institutions are now operating in the market. Six British conglomerates will compete with the larger American and Japanese investment banks in providing the full range of international financial services. They are Barclays de Zoete Wedd, NatWest Investment Bank, Midland Montagu, Morgan Grenfell, Kleinwort Benson and Mercury International. Most of the other UK firms will operate in specialist areas or stick to traditional lines of business.

The total market capitalisation of the UK market stood at £4441.8 billion at the end of 1989. Turnover in the equity market rose from £105.6 billion during 1985 to £246.2 billion during 1989. Gilt market turnover increased by about one-third, from £261.5 billion in 1985 to £531.5 billion in 1989. The number of personal shareholders has remained stable over the last three years, despite the result of the government's privatisation programme. Share ownership is dominated by institutional investors, pension funds, insurance companies, unit and investment trusts.

Table 1.3 illustrates that institutional investors accounted for 54.6 per cent of the total market value of listed ordinary shares in 1987; the figures may not be exact, but they are a good indication of the order of magnitude. Although this proportion of market share has probably diminished slightly since then (because of the privatisation programme), they are undoubtedly still the main investors.

Table 1.3   *Share ownership by investor type, 1963, 1984 and 1987* (percentages)

	1963	1984	1987
Pension funds/insurance/unit trusts/investment trusts	27.8	60.0	54.6
Charities/industrial/commercial/ government/overseas	13.5	18.0	23.8
Individuals	58.7	22.0	21.6
Total	100.0	100.0	100.0

Source: Hildeburn (1986), *GT Guide to World Equity Markets* (London: Euromoney) and Stock Exchange Quality of Markets Quarterly, 1987

As has already been mentioned, commercial, merchant and foreign banks now own broker-dealers, and members of other stock exchanges have also established broker-dealers in the United Kingdom. This does not explain, however, the strength of the foreign banks, including investment banks and overseas securities houses in the London market. The main reason why London has attracted over 570 foreign institutions is because it is the capital of the euromarkets. In 1987 turnover on the eurobond market was more than $3 trillion and the eurocurrency deposit market is even larger; 1987 turnover totalled over $4 trillion. Other markets include the eurocommercial paper and euro-equity market. Most of the activity in the markets is wholesale and, as a result, the operators are typically large organisations, like banks, securities houses, institutional investors or commercial companies.

Various other markets have played an important role in the developing structure of the UK financial system during the 1980s. These include:

1. Unlisted Securities Market (USM),
2. Third Tier Market,

3. Over-the-counter (OTC) Market,
4. sterling commercial paper (SCP) market,
5. London International Financial Futures Exchange (LIFFE),
6. foreign exchange market.

The Unlisted Securities Market was introduced in November 1980 as a junior tier of the official Stock Exchange. The main aim of the market was to provide funds for smaller and/or young companies, which could use the listing as a stepping-stone before advancing to the more rigorously regulated environment of a full listing. Since 1980 over 70 companies have graduated to the main market. In 1986 over 400 companies' securities were traded in this market and, since its inception, over £1 billion has been raised.

The 'Third Market' was established in January 1987 to complement a full listing on the USM. Its object was to provide venture capital for new young (greenfield) growth companies that do not fulfil the requirements for trading on other markets. Companies are only required to provide a one-year trading record in order to obtain a listing. Eight companies joined on the opening day. The 'Third Market' poses a substantial threat to the long-established Over-the-Counter (OTC) market. In fact, the Stock Exchange has admitted that the growth in this market was a major factor behind the decision to establish a new third-tier market. By the end of 1986, 153 companies were still quoted on the OTC, which was effectively unregulated up until the introduction of the Financial Services Act in 1986.

Another recent development was the introduction of the sterling commercial paper (SCP) market, which became operational on 20 May 1986; by early June borrowing programmes totalling £1.7 billion had been announced by 14 companies. The market has many distinctive attractions for well-rated industrial and commercial companies. Through by-passing the banking system, they can obtain funds more cheaply on the sterling CP market, and they can also invest funds more profitably when they are in surplus. The progress of this market since its inception has been steady rather than rapid, partly because official requirements deterred some potential borrowers, and partly because others remained unconvinced that issuing commercial paper was the cheapest way to borrow. The SCP market was given a boost in the 1989 Budget when the Chancellor of the Exchequer announced a number of changes to the regulations governing the market. Companies with minimum net assets of £25 million and which have a listing of either debt or equity on the International Stock Exchange in London, or whose shares are traded on the USM are now eligible to issue SCP. Companies that do not have listings but fulfil the net asset requirements will also be able to issue SCP subject to them providing additional information to the International Stock Exchange. Overseas companies may also access this market if they are listed on major overseas exchanges and fulfil the net asset and information requirements. In addition, companies may issue SCP if the paper is guaranteed by a company meeting the net worth and UK listing requirements, or by a bank authorised under the 1987 Banking Act. Banks, building societies, insurance companies and various international organisations are now eligible to issue SCP. The 1989 Budget proposals maintained the original minimum required maturity of 7 days but extended the maximum from 1 year to 5 years. Minimum note denomination is reduced from £500 000 to £100 000. By mid-1989 there were 150 SCP programmes outstanding, totalling £13 billion with around £4 billion in issue. Issuers to date tend to be large multinationals and medium-sized national companies but it is hoped the new legislation will attract a significant number of medium and small-sized firms to the market.

The London International Financial Futures Exchange (LIFFE) has established itself at the forefront of European futures and options exchanges. Since its inception in September 1982 its membership has increased from 200 to 373 seats, with turnover exceeding 60 000 contracts a day equal to about 50 per cent of the value of stock transactions. Although comparatively small compared with the Chicago exchange, LIFFE's exceptional growth has shown that there was a need for this kind of market. In addition the London Traded Options Market offers investors the opportunity to deal in share options of over twenty named companies.

London is an amalgam of financial markets dealing in a sophisticated range of capital and money market instruments. Two additional markets that also play a significant role in the financial system are the foreign exchange market and Lloyd's. London is the centre of world foreign exchange markets. The average daily foreign exchange turnover during March 1989 amounted to $187 billion in London, compared with $129 billion in New York and $115 billion in Tokyo. The dominance of London in this market has undoubtedly improved the international flavour of the operations of UK-based financial institutions.

Lloyd's of London, with an annual premium income of $8 billion in 1987, is mainly a reinsurance market, depending on North America for approximately half of its business. It is by far the largest reinsurance market in the world. Both reinsurance and other insurance business is conducted in the market. Clients that require insurance have to deal with brokers, who negotiate the terms for the insurance contract with underwriters. Underwriters compete for business on behalf of the members (known as 'names') of various syndicates. By the end of 1986 there were 216 syndicates with more than 30 000 members.

Given the new regulatory climate and the importance of the euromarkets in London, most large domestic and foreign banks offer a broad range of financial services from international and eurobusiness to retail broking services. Clearing banks as well as some building societies can now sell shares through their branches as well as offer integrated investment management services. The four main clearers offer private client investment and retail stockbroking facilities and offer unit trust business through their branch networks. In general, because of the above developments, traditional demarcation lines between commercial banks, savings banks, building societies, insurance companies and other financial institutions will continue to erode. It is expected that a whole range of financial institutions will offer comprehensive securities and brokerage business in the near future.

References and further reading

Child Report (1984) *Payment Clearing Systems: Review of Organisation, Management and Control*, Member banks of the Bankers Clearing House (London: Banking Information Service).

Hildeburn, G. (1986) GT Guide to World Equity Markets (London: Euromoney).

Struthers, J. and Speight, H. (1986) *Money: Institutions, Theory and Policy* (London: Longmans).

CHAPTER 2

ANALYSIS OF THE EVOLUTION OF UK MARKETS AND FINANCIAL INTERMEDIARIES

INTRODUCTION

The UK financial system has experienced rapid structural changes since the early 1980s. Many evolutionary forces have been at work guiding these developments. The volatile market environment throughout this era, coupled with the heightened competitive awareness of financial institutions and the worldwide trend towards the deregulation of financial systems, resulted in a new 'dynamic' in the UK financial markets. The main aspects of these developments are discussed in this chapter.

ROLE OF FINANCIAL INTERMEDIATION

Any analysis of the evolutionary forces moulding the structure of a financial system must first identify the main functions of such a system. These are outlined generally by Llewellyn (1985) as follows:

1. to provide mechanisms for the disposal of savings or financial surpluses and the financing of investment or financial deficits
2. to bridge the different portfolio preferences of surplus and deficit agents by offering the depositor a different type of asset from that acquired by the financial intermediary
3. to allocate funds to the most efficient uses
4. to enable risks to be diversified and transferred from ultimate savers
5. to enable changes to be made to the structure of portfolios

Typically, those systems that provide an efficient payments mechanism, broad intermediation and asset transmutation capabilities and a diversified portfolio of financial services and products are the hallmark of a well-developed financial system. Rybczynski (1984) identifies three stages of evolution in financial systems: the bank-orientated stage, market-orientated and strongly market-orientated.

The bank-orientated phase in this model is characterised by the dominance of the banks in the intermediation process. During this phase the main role of financial intermediaries, and especially banks, is to provide non-marketable loans to firms in order to fulfil their working capital requirements. Funding is mainly through the collection of retail deposits. The risk capital needs of the private sector are obtained mainly from firms' retained profits. Other financial intermediaries, such as insurance companies and pension funds, lend long-term to governments and firms.

The second stage of development, the 'market-orientated' phase begins when the capital market starts to play a more important role in the financial system, the long-term requirements of surplus and deficit agents being met by the increased use of long-term marketable loans; there is generally a wider availability of risk capital (equity) instruments. Finally, Rybczynski (1984, p. 38) states that the 'strongly market-orientated' phase is characterised by the 'marked increase in the breadth and depth of capital markets, rapid expansion in the scope of credit markets, a blurring of the dividing lines between the credit and capital markets, and a sharp increase in the reliance of banks and depository institutions on funds obtained through credit markets rather than from ultimate savers'. In addition, markets in new financial instruments such as futures, options and the like, will emerge during this phase, providing a broader range of services to both surplus and deficit agents.

There is no doubt that the UK financial system is now 'strongly market-orientated'. Demarcation lines between institutions, markets and even regulatory bodies have become markedly blurred over the last five years. Two forms of 'structural diffusion' illustrate the aforementioned phenomena: 'institutional structural diffusion' and 'market structural diffusion'. The former relates to the broadening product and service facilities offered by a wider range of financial institutions. Financial intermediaries that traditionally dominated various areas of service provision – namely building societies for housing finance, insurance companies for insurance products, stockbrokers for broking facilities, and so on – are having to compete with other financial institutions in areas which at one time were almost considered sacrosanct to specialist institutions. The widening of the product bases of financial institutions, despecialisation, has resulted in a greater variety of firms doing business at finer rates in a more competitive market environment. Retail and wholesale banking markets have become more integrated in the United Kingdom during recent years. As demarcation lines break down between both markets and institutions, and as financial information becomes more readily available and adaptable through the new technologies, the role of the financial system will become enhanced by its ability to operate more efficiently and offer more risk-hedging and management possibilities.

EVOLUTIONARY FORCES DURING THE 1980s

Market environment and demand factors

The more volatile market environment within which UK financial institutions have operated during the last decade has had a marked impact on the structure of the financial system and on the attitudes of savers and investors. The increased volatility of interest and exchange rates, coupled with inflationary pressures and a general economic depression in the late 1970s and early 1980s, encouraged surplus and deficit agents to revise their portfolio positions. It also encouraged the government to introduce legislation which fostered competition between financial intermediaries (structural deregulation) and also stimulated policies to restrain monetary growth.

During 1979 exchange controls were abolished, and this encouraged the private sector to invest more readily in overseas securities and other investments. Although the abolition of these controls was expected to render a once for all stock adjustment, in fact it led to a 'new dynamic' in competition between financial institutions. In addition, the abolition of exchange controls made certain aspects of monetary policy ineffective. The corset or supplementary special deposits (SSD) scheme was a direct method of monetary control encompassing the threat of a 'call' by the authorities on the banks' deposits if their business grew too quickly. After the abolition of exchange controls, banks found it easy to disintermediate around the corset restrictions; this method of direct monetary control ended in June 1980. The introduction in March 1980 of the Medium Term Financial Strategy (MTFS) aimed to restrain monetary growth by specifying targets for various money aggregates. The objective was to influence longer-term expectations about nominal income and monetary growth.

In the inflationary environment that had persisted throughout the late 1970s industrial and commercial companies moved away from raising fixed-rate funds through the capital markets and borrowed more heavily from the banks. As the economy worsened in the early 1980s, traditional lines of intermediation increased (greater indirect financial intermediation), highlighted by the marked decline in money velocities after 1980. (Only M0 the narrowest monetary aggregate, increased during this period.) As corporate customers looked increasingly towards banks for their financing needs, the banks began to obtain an increasing share of their funds from the wholesale money markets.

In 1982 the Third World debt crisis temporarily led the main international operators in the market to reappraise the situation. With the resultant decline in the creditworthiness of banks througout the world and the subsequent pressure on 'on-balance sheet' lending margins, top quality international corporate customers began to disintermediate their banks by issuing securities directly on the capital market. Nevertheless, this trend towards securitisation was an international corporate banking phenomenon and did not initially stem the growth in traditional corporate lending in the United Kingdom.

Substantial changes have also occurred in the provision of retail financial services. A noticeable feature of retail banking in the early 1980s was the move in 1981 of the major clearers into the house mortgage market, which traditionally had been left as a virtual monopoly of building societies. This altered a long-standing feature of UK banking, and it eroded further the traditional specialist division in lending activities between banks and building societies.

Table 2.1 shows that the retail banks' market share of net lending for house purchase increased from a lowly 5 per cent in 1978 to 35.9 per cent in 1982, the peak of the banks' share of net mortgage lending. The market share of banks has declined since then to approximately one-quarter of the total. On the liabilities side, the banks' share of UK residents' deposits has been on a decline since the early 1960s, although recently the clearing banks have marginally increased their significance in the retail deposit market. The opposite holds for the building societies whose market share passed that of the clearing banks in 1975. Table 2.2 highlights these salient features.

Table 2.1 *Net Lending for House Purchase by Retail Banks and Building Societies, 1978–87* (percentages of total net lending by all lenders)

	1978	1980	1982	1987
Retail banks	5.0	5.2	35.9	27.2
Building societies	94.6	79.0	57.6	51.4
Other lenders	0.4	14.1	6.5	21.4
Total	100.0	100.0	100.0	100.0

Note: Retail banks are London and Scottish banks' groups and the Trustee Savings Bank
Source: CLSB, *Abstract of Banking Statistics*, vol. 5, May 1988

Table 2.2 *Distribution of Deposits: Holdings of UK Residents with Principal Institutions in the United Kingdom* (percentages of total UK residents' sterling deposits)

	1978	1980	1982	1987
London and Scottish clearing banks	38.9	39.1	33.6	37.9
Other UK monetary sector institutions	12.1	12.0	18.5	16.3
Total UK monetary sector institutions	51.0	51.1	52.2	54.2
Building societies	41.4	41.3	42.4	41.6
Others (National Savings, Treasury bills, Local authority temporary debt and certificates of tax deposits)	7.6	7.6	5.4	4.2
Total	100.0	100.0	100.0	100.0

Source: Calculated from CLSB, *Abstract of Banking Statistics*, vol. 5, May 1988

As the building societies had previously rationed mortgages, the entry of the main clearing banks into the market meant that demand could now be fulfilled. Increased competition between the banks and building societies fostered a broader range of retail banking products that enhanced the liquidity position of building society deposits in particular.

The increase in individuals' deposit liabilities during the 1980s, however, has had only a small impact on the substantial increase in total banking sector deposits as monitored by the major monetary aggregate, sterling M3. The rapid increase in this aggregate was attributable to the increased growth of the deposits of industrial and commercial companies and non-bank financial intermediaries. Over the last decade probably the most significant factor in the portfolio behaviour of individuals, industrial and commercial companies and non-bank financial intermediaries is the simultaneous build-up of debt and liquid asset holdings.

A recent paper (Bank of England, 1986) attributed the personal sector's simultaneous desire for increased debt and liquidity to the changing behaviour of financial intermediaries. Amongst other things, increased competition between banks and building societies in the retail deposits market during the early 1980s had the effect of improving the attractiveness of personal sector liquid asset holdings relative to other assets. As a result, a substantial part of the increase in personal sector liquidity since 1980, which is mainly held with building societies rather than banks, can be attributed to a redistribution of personal sector assets as a response to changes in the behaviour of financial intermediaries. The altered portfolio position of industrial and commercial companies was attributed to various changes in tax treatments – namely, lower corporation tax and relief on leasing activities (no longer available) as well as the boom in takeover and merger business. The portfolio position of the non-bank financial intermediaries altered mainly because of the personal credit boom and the resultant increase in bank borrowing to finance this business. An increasing proportion of this sector's liquid assets is in the form of bank deposits.

As mentioned earlier, an important factor influencing the portfolio positions of individuals and companies in the post-war development of the UK financial system has been the taxation system. During the last decade, the most notable features have been the preferential tax treatment allowed on life assurance and pension products, tax relief on mortgages, capital gains tax benefits on unit and investment trusts and various incentives on government debt and national savings. Whether the tax treatment of different forms of savings and/or investment is justifiable or not, the tax system has helped to discriminate in favour of certain financial products and services. Tax relief on mortgage finance and personal pension schemes is still significant.

The portfolio preferences and general demands of the users of financial services have also become much more sophisticated. On the retail financial services side, the changing demography and financial status of customers mean that all institutions operating in the market are being faced with a retailing challenge. Retail customers are also becoming generally more sophisticated under the pressures of intensive marketing. Retail demands are becoming more sophisticated, and customer loyalty is decreasing. Customers are demanding more services, better information and, most importantly, value for money. The traditional providers of retail financial services are having to alter their cultural orientation more towards retailing and marketing. Through market segmentation, product differentiation and accurate packaging, financial institutions are offering services in designated 'target' markets – one parent families, high net-worth individuals (HNWIs), house buyers and the like.

Similar forces have probably been more prevalent for a longer period of time in the corporate and wholesale financial services sector. This market has always provided a relatively specialised service, offering both cross-selling and relationship pricing opportunities. With the emergence of financial innovations such as note issuance facilities (NIFs), revolving underwriting facilities (RUFs), swaps, futures, options and the like, the demands of corporate and financial institutions' treasury departments are becoming much more sophisticated. As has already been mentioned, the largest non-financial corporations are now able to enter the financial markets direct, thus decreasing their demand for traditional intermediation services.

Any analysis of the environmental and demand factors that have moulded the UK financial system would not be complete without a mention of the regulatory forces that have encouraged change. We have already touched upon the abolition of exchange controls in 1979 that led to a 'new dynamic' in the market, as well as various other macroeconomic policies that influenced the behaviour of financial institutions. In addition to these, 'Big Bang' on 27 October

1986 abolished restrictive practices on the trading floor of the London Stock Exchange by getting rid of fixed commissions, single capacity and the jobbers' oligopoly in the gilts markets. Soon after, trading moved off the Stock Exchange floor, and most transactions are now undertaken through telecommunications links. The main reasons for these developments were to enhance the competitive efficiency of the domestic capital market as well as to consolidate London's position as a truly international centre. Foreign banks and securities houses had begun to air their dissatisfaction about fixed commissions on securities transactions, and some found it cheaper to trade in UK company shares in the United States through American Depository Receipts (ADRs). Threats to move their business elsewhere also helped to concentrate minds. Trading volume increased rapidly after 'Big Bang' and commission rates have dropped dramatically, especially for the institutional investors.

In addition to the deregulation of the capital market, the 1986 Building Societies Act extended the traditional role of the building societies so that they are now able to offer a broader range of banking, investment, insurance and other non-financial products. Although their business is still dominated at present by mortgage lending and the taking of retail savings deposits, some of the larger institutions have been given official access to the centralised clearing system, and all but one of the top ten societies offer unsecured personal loans. The new legislation will no doubt intensify the breakdown of demarcation lines between traditional banking and building society business. Overall, it is clear that UK financial intermediaries have had to offer a wider and more sophisticated range of financial services, more attuned to user needs, in a highly competitive market environment. Structural deregulation (the liberalisation of financial institutions and markets) has been pervasive throughout the whole of the UK financial system. Financial and non-financial intermediaries are now able to compete on more level terms in the market. The competitive environment has helped spawn business in new financial instruments ranging from futures, options and CP to asset-backed securities traded in both the domestic and international arenas. There is no doubt that the forces of deregulation, competition and innovation will continue to have a substantial impact in moulding the UK financial system.

Supply factors

The major evolutionary forces that have operated on the supply side of the UK financial system are as follows:

1. growth in the variety of financial institutions operating in a broader range of markets and the subsequent decline in business demarcation lines,
2. conglomeration, specialisation and the wider use of agency and franchising arrangements, together with the forming of groups and associations,
3. internationalisation of financial markets,
4. the increased importance of pension funds, insurance companies, building societies, and non-banking financial institutions in general,
5. competition, deregulation, technology, innovation, and social and economic factors.

During the 1980s there has been an ever-increasing range of financial and non-financial institutions offering a broad range of services in the UK marketplace.

Non-bank financial intermediaries now offer a host of traditional retail banking and other consumer financial services. Foreign institutions have consolidated their position in the wholesale as well as corporate banking markets; some even offer a limited range of retail financial services. Tables 2.3 – 2.5 illustrate the variety of products offered by some of the major groups. As UK and foreign banks make major inroads into the securities and brokerage business, building societies are now allowed to offer a wider range of banking services following the 1986 Building Societies Act. Virtually all non-bank financial intermediaries, as shown in Table 2.5, offer some form of deposit-taking facility. These trends confirm the earlier picture that traditional demarcation lines between different lines of business are breaking down fast.

A recent report on innovations in international banking (Bank for International Settlements, 1986) stated that increased competition in financial markets has come in two forms: between different national financial systems and between banks and non-bank financial institutions within the domestic financial system.

Table 2.3 *Clearing Banks and UK Merchant Banks after 'Big Bang'*

Banks/group	Stock exchange capitalisation	Main purchases or partners in London	A	B	C	D	E	F	G	H	I	J	K	L	M	N	O	P	Q	R	S	T	U	V	W	X	Y	Z
UK Clearing banks																												
Barclays	3,570	de Zoete & Bevan (S) Wedd Durlacher Mordaunt (J) Barclays Merchant Bank (M)	X	X	X	X	X	X	X	X	X		X	X	X	X	X	X	X	X	X	X	X		X		X	X
Lloyds	2,236	Black Horse Agencies (E) Lloyds Merchant Bank (M)					X	X	X	X	X	X	X		X	X	X	X	X	X	X	X	X	X	X	X	X	X
Midland	1,291	Samuel Montagu (M) W. Greenwell (S)	X	X	X	X	X	X	X	X	X		X	X	X	X	X	X	X		X	X	X		X			X
National Westminster	3,737	Fielding, Newson-Smith (S) County Bank (M) Bisgood Bishop (J)	X	X	X	X	X	X	X	X	X	X	X	X	X	X	X	X	X	X	X	X	X	X	X	X	X	X
UK merchant banks																												
Barings	—	Wilson & Watford (J)	X	X	X	X	X	X	X	X			X	X	X		X	X	X	X	X	X			X		X	X
Hambros	381	Strauss Turnbull (S) Mann & Co. (E) Bairstow Eves (S)	X	X		X	X		X	X	X	X	X	X	X	X	X	X	X	X	X	X	X	X	X	X	X	X
Hill Samuel	332	Wood Mackenzie (S)	X	X	X	X	X	X	X	X	X	X	X	X	X	X	X		X	X	X	X	X	X	X	X	X	X
Kleinwort Benson	479	Grieveson Grant (S) Charlesworth & Co. (J)	X	X	X	X	X	X		X	X	X	X	X	X	X	X		X	X	X	X	X		X		X	
Mercantile House	233	Laing & Cruickshank (S) Alexanders Discount (D)	X	X	X	X				X	X	X	X	X	X	X	X	X	X	X	X	X						
Morgan Grenfell	664	Pember & Boyle (S) Pinchin Denny (J)	X	X	X	X	X	X	X	X	X	X	X	X	X	X	X	X	X			X	X			X		X
N.M. Rothschild	—	Smith Bros. (J)	X	X		X	X	X		X	X	X	X	X	X	X	X	X	X	X	X		X	X	X		X	
Schroders	160	Helbert Wagg, Anderson, Bryce Villiers (S)	X	X		X	X	X	X	X	X	X	X	X	X	X	X	X	X	X	X	X	X	X	X	X	X	X
S.G. Warburg (Mercury International)	399	Akroyd & Smithers (J) Rowe & Pitman (S) Mullens (S)	X	X	X	X	X	X	X	X	X	X	X	X	X	X	X	X	X	X	X	X	X			X		

Key:
A UK equities market making
B International equities market making
C Gilts primary dealing
D Futures, options and swaps
E Eurobond market making
F Eurobond underwriting
G Eurocommercial paper
H Sterling commercial paper
I US Treasury securities market making
J Equity issues
K Retail stockbroking
L Retail banking
M Wholesale banking
N Foreign exchange
O Mergers and acquisitions
P Commodities
Q Bullion
R Consumer finance
S Unit trusts
T Fund management
U Private client investment
V Estate agents
W Mortages (£)
X Commercial property
Y Venture capital
Z Insurance

Notes:
(C) commercial bank
(D) discount house
(E) estate agent
(J) jobber ﹀
(M) merchant bank
(S) stockbroker

Source: *Economist* (1986), 'Big Bang brief – the home teams', vol. 300, no. 7461, 30 August–5 September 1986

Table 2.4 *Top 20 UK Building Societies: Profile of Services*
(Excluding Mortgages)

Services	1	2	3	4	5	6	7	8	9	10	11	12	13	14	15	16
Halifax	X			X		X		X		X					X	X
Abbey National	X			X	X	X	X	X				X	V			X
Nationwide	X	X		X	X		X	X	X	X	X	X	A	X	X	X
Alliance & Leicester				X	X	X	X	X	X			X	X	X		X
Leeds Permanent				X	X	X	X	X	X					X	X	X
Woolwich Equitable	X			X	X	X	X	X						X	X	X
Anglia*	X		X	X		X	X	X	X		X	X	X	X		X
National & Provincial	X		X	X	X	X	X	X	X	X	X		X	X		X
Bradford & Bingley	X			X		X		X	X		X	X				X
Britannia	X			X	X	X	X	X	X	X	X	X	V			X
Cheltenham & Gloucester								X					V			X
Bristol & West				X	X		X	X							X	X
Yorkshire*				X			X	X								X
Gateway*				X			X									X
Northern Rock			X			X							X		X	X
Town & Country				X	X	X		X	X				X	X	X	X
Midshires	X	X		X	X	X	X			X		X				X
Coventry				X		X	X	X	X			X			X	X
Guardian*																
Skipton			X			X									X	X

Notes: * to be announced

V Visa

A Access

Since 1987 the Nationwide has merged with the Anglia, Woolwich has acquired Gateway, Cheltenham and Gloucester have acquired the Guardian and Abbey National has been publicly listed.

Key:

1	PEPs (personal equity plans)		9	Standing orders
2	Unit trusts		10	Foreign exchange
3	Share dealing		11	Direct debit
4	ATMs		12	Personal pensions
5	Cheque book		13	Credit card
6	Personal loans		14	Overdraft
7	Traveller's cheques		15	Estate agency
8	Direct payment of wages		16	Insurance

Source: Retail Banker International, 1987

Table 2.5 *'Retail Banking' and Other Consumer Financial Services of Non-bank Financial Intermediaries*

	Services								
Type of intermediary	*A*	*B*	*C*	*D*	*E*	*F*	*G*	*H*	*I*
Insurance companies			X	X		X	X	X	
Stockbrokers	X			X	X	X		X	
Unit trusts	X			X		X			
Retailers		X			X		X		
Pension fund/investment trusts				X X X				X	
Travel service companies	X	X	X	X	X	X	X	X	X
Overseas investment banks	X		X	X	X	X		X	X
Offshore institutions				X	X	X			
Postal banks	X	X	X	X			X		
Others		X	X	X			X		

Source: Middleton (1987)

Key:
A Current account facilities
B Consumer credit
C Loans and mortgages
D Deposit taking
E Securities dealing
F Investment management and unit trusts
G Insurance products
H Financial advice
I Other products and services

To cope with the more intense competitive environment throughout the 1980s, banks and other financial intermediaries have sought to broaden their product bases and expertise by acquiring and/or establishing subsidiaries to form large conglomerates.

Conglomeration is a noticeable feature of the largest UK commercial banks. The recent deregulation of the UK capital market serves to illustrate this point when the largest two clearing banks purchased both broking and jobbing firms to complement their merchant banking subsidiaries. This phenomenon, however, is not confined to UK institutions alone, and given the current trend towards the globalisation of financial markets (especially capital and money markets), it is widely accepted that organisations wishing to be involved in the full range of financial services must have a corresponding global coverage if they are to be successful. This is a further 'boost' to the conglomeration trend. Nevertheless, this trend towards 'universal' financial service provision is probably within the capability of only the largest financial institutions.

What has also emerged in the UK financial system is a whole range of specialists, agents and franchisers, groups and associations that either aim to fill niche markets or hope to broaden their range of services by forming links with other organisations. For example, prior to 'Big Bang', Cazenove, one of London's major brokers, resisted all takeover advances, and it has preserved its traditional role in the market. Similarly, N. M. Rothschild, the merchant banking firm, is sticking to traditional lines of business, although some of its contemporaries have broadened their activities.

Smaller financial intermediaries have been able to fulfil specialist roles in various ways, mainly as agents of outside groupings. An example is the Bank of Scotland, one of the smaller clearing banks, which has specialised in providing current account services for building societies and other organisations that were previously not able to do so legally. Most building societies act as agents for insurance companies by selling policies through their extensive branch networks. Some small institutions have operated as outside partners for the development of new systems dependent on information technology: Nottingham Building Society's home banking system, for example.

Finally, agency and/or franchising agreements seem to be of particular interest to small and medium-sized institutions, because these offer the opportunity to provide well-known products and services in localised markets. Link-ups with other organisations might well reduce the vulnerability of small to medium-sized institutions which could be potential acquisition targets. The trend towards conglomeration and universal service provision may be counterbalanced to some extent by the increased formation of groupings and specialisations within the financial system.

The overriding trend towards the liberalisation of worldwide capital and money markets over the last decade, coupled with the rise of international banking business, has resulted in the internationalisation of the major financial markets. Nowhere is this more prevalent than in London. Given the disinflationary environment over the last four years, investors all over the world have been encouraged to purchase more securities than ever before. With the general deregulatory climate, innovations in swap arrangements and declining interest rates, this has also led to a marked boom in eurobond issues as well as dealings in other financial instruments such as euronotes.

The internationalisation of the UK financial markets goes hand in hand with the phenomenon of securitisation. The business of corporate financial intermediation is changing, and the days when domestic institutions served their clients through their branch networks are exclusively disappearing. More and more retail funds are being channelled into the securities subsidiaries of the large financial institutions. Parent companies (especially banks) are watching their securities subsidiaries grow on the funds provided from their retail operations. Furthermore, most of this business is transacted with overseas investors. These developments have significance not only for the internationalisation and integration of securities markets but also for the structure of the UK financial system itself.

Another important evolutionary factor influencing the supply of financial services has been the increase in importance of pension funds, insurance companies, building societies and non-bank financial institutions in general. As has already been mentioned, the preferential tax treatment applied to products and services offered by these suppliers has encouraged their substantial growth. The total assets of insurance and pension fund companies exceeded those of the clearing banks in 1989, and building societies have had a larger market share of retail sterling deposits since the mid-1970s. In addition, the pension funds and insurance companies are by far the most important investors in securities in the United Kingdom. Their predominance in this market will probably continue, given the present internationalisation and securitisation trends.

Building societies have lost market share in the domestic mortgage market since the early 1980s, but the continuous concentration in the industry (i.e. increasing market share of the largest institutions), coupled with the liberating Building Societies Act of 1986, should help to redress the balance through the enhanced ability of the societies to develop new lines of business. Other non-bank financial intermediaries, such as finance houses, factoring and leasing companies and the like, have also grown considerably over the last ten years. Most of these, in fact, are wholly-owned subsidiaries of the major London clearing banks (LCBs). Their growth has been compounded given the trend towards conglomeration.

Finally, the evolutionary forces affecting the supply side of the UK financial system are sometimes subsumed under catch-all categories which include competition, deregulation, technology, innovation and social and economic factors. Aspects of these forces have already been mentioned elsewhere in this chapter. The increased institutional and market structural diffusion experienced over the last decade, fostered by deregulation, advances in technology and financial innovation, have helped to create a more competitive financial system. Factors such as the growth and internationalisation of the securities industry, the increased amount of off-balance sheet business undertaken by banks, and the decline in demarcation lines between traditional business areas have all been nurtured by the aforementioned forces. There is no doubt that the system is now much more market-orientated than it was ten years ago.

References and further reading

Bank for International Settlements (1986) *Recent Innovations in International Banking*, April (Basle: BIS).

Bank of England (1986) 'Financial change and broad money', *Bank of England Quarterly Bulletin*, December, vol. 26, no. 4.

Llewellyn, D.T. (1985) *The Evolution of the British Financial System: Gilbert Lectures on Banking* (London: Institute of Bankers).

Middleton, P. (1987) 'Are non-banks winning in retail financial services?', *International Journal of Bank Marketing*, vol. 5, no. 1.

Rybczynski, T.M. (1984) 'The UK financial system in transition', *National Westminster Bank Quarterly Review*, November.

CHAPTER 3

CLAIMS, FINANCIAL INTERMEDIATION AND THE DEVELOPMENT OF FINANCIAL SYSTEMS

INTRODUCTION

To understand how financial institutions work it is important to understand the financial environment in which they operate. As the financial environment changes (perhaps because people become more wealthy and therefore save more), so financial institutions must adapt and change if they are to remain successful. So an understanding of the basic 'mechanics' by which the desire of savers to earn a return on their funds creates profitable opportunities for financial institutions, is central to the existence of financial systems. This chapter deals with the way in which financial institutions are able to gather savers' funds and the use to which they put these funds.

FINANCIAL CLAIMS AND FINANCIAL INTERMEDIATION

Financial claims

A financial claim is a claim to the payment of a future sum of money and/or a periodic payment of money. In general, a financial claim carries an obligation on the issuer to pay interest periodically and to redeem the claim at a stated value in one of three ways:

1. on demand,
2. after the giving of a stated period of notice,
3. on a definite date or within a range of dates.

Financial claims are generated whenever an act of borrowing takes place. Borrowing occurs whenever an economic unit's (whether it be an individual, household, company, etc.) total expenditure exceeds its total receipts. (Note that borrowers are generally referred to as *deficit units* whereas lenders are known as *surplus units*.) Examples of financial claims, taken from Revell (1975) would include:

1. *Money* – financial claims that act solely as a medium of exchange
   (a) notes and coins,
   (b) bank current accounts.

2. *Wholesale near-money* – large denomination financial claims. Individual wholesale deposits are usually greater than £50 000:
   (a) secondary bank time deposits,
   (b) certificates of deposit,
   (c) local authority deposits,
   (d) finance house deposits.

3. *Retail near-money* – small denomination financial claims:
   (a) deposit bank deposit accounts,
   (b) building society deposits,
   (c) savings bank deposits,
   (d) other national savings.

4. *Bills* – short-term claims, issued at a discount and redeemed at par value:
   (a) Treasury bills
   (b) Commercial bills

5. *Bonds* - long-term claims, issued by businesses and governments as a way of borrowing long-term funds. Repayable on maturity and pay a fixed rate of interest (coupon):
   (a) british government,
   (b) local authority,
   (c) company debentures.

6. *Shares* – financial claims issued by a joint stock company. These claims are evidence that the holder partly owns the issuing company. Income is variable:
   (a) preference,

(b) ordinary,
(c) unit trust units (mutual trusts).

7. *Loans* – claims advanced by financial institutions used to finance investments and current consumption:
   (a) bank advances,
   (b) instalment credit,
   (c) house purchase,
   (d) other.

8. *Life policies* – financial claims that insures clients for loss caused by specific accidents and also acts as an investment medium.

In short, a financial claim is any form of financial asset. Note that this listing is by no means comprehensive and it is used purely for illustrative purposes. During the course of this text many of the aforementioned will become familiar.

Financial intermediation

Financial intermediation is an essential feature of the borrowing-lending process. It bridges the gap between borrowers (deficit units) and lenders (surplus units) and reconciles their often incompatible needs and objectives. Two types of barriers to the financing process can be identified. They are:

1. The difficulty and expense of matching the complex needs of individual borrowers and lenders.
2. The incompatibility of the financial needs and objectives of borrowers and lenders.

The lender is looking for safety and *liquidity* (the ease of converting a financial claim into cash without loss of capital value) and the borrower may find it difficult to promise either. Financial institutions can reconcile these needs by offering suppliers of funds safety and liquidity by using funds deposited by surplus units for loans and investments with varying degrees of *risk* and *liquidity*. Figure 3.1 helps to illustrate the positioning of the financial intermediary between borrowers and lenders.

Figure 3.1 *The Link Between Borrowers and Lenders*

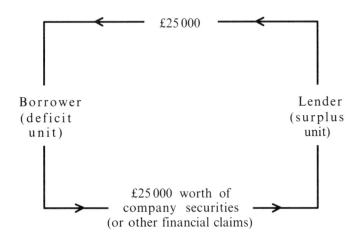

Figure 3.1 shows a situation where deficit units borrow directly from lenders. No financial intermediary enters the relationship. An example of this kind might be where a saver decides to buy a new issue of shares in a company. In Figure 3.2 the lender does not provide funds directly to the borrower but places funds with a financial intermediary and in return has a deposit or claim on the financial intermediary (in this case £25 000 worth of deposits). The financial intermediary can then on-lend these funds to borrowers who in return provide some form of security (in this case £25 000 worth of company shares) to ensure that the loan will (hopefully) be repaid. (Note: In this hypothetical case a new issue of shares is given by the borrower to the lender as security. Buying shares in a company is a form of lending to a company only in the case of new issues, etc. There is no secondary market for the shares.) If you find this difficult to understand, just consider the assurances you would have to make to your bank manager if you wished to take out any form of loan.

Figure 3.2   *Financial Intermediation*

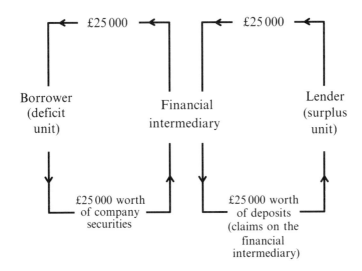

The need for financial intermediation is brought about by various circumstances and requirements which generally apply to lenders and borrowers:

1. Lenders wish to minimise risks, ie they hope to minimise the eventuality that the borrower is unable to repay.
2. Lenders require convenience and liquidity.
3. Lenders prefer to lend for a short period of time.
4. Borrowers require funds at a particular point in time, for a fixed period and at the lowest possible cost.
5. Borrowers prefer to borrow for a long period of time.

Financial intermediation provides the mechanism in which the needs of both the lender and the borrower can be met. Referring back to Figure 3.2 you will see that the financial intermediary provides the lender with a different type of asset (£25 000 worth of deposits) compared with the case where no intermediation takes place (where the asset was £25 000 worth of company securities).

The lenders' asset (or financial claim) is more liquid than before and the borrowers funds are more certain. In addition, the financial intermediary has on-lent funds in exchange for an asset (£25 000 worth of company securities) which is less liquid than the corresponding liability (£25 000 worth of deposits) in its own balance sheet. It is important to remember that in general, the assets of a financial intermediary are less liquid than its liabilities.

Financial intermediaries can give their suppliers of funds long-term contracts and lend on short-term contracts, or they can borrow short and lend long. Their ability to match apparently inconsistent types of financial contracts is sometimes called the asset-transmutation effect.

THE DEVELOPMENT OF THE FINANCIAL SYSTEM

To gain a significant insight into the types and structures of financial markets and institutions, and the inter-relationships between them and the various categories of financial claims which they issue, then it is best to approach the question of financial structure within a historical context. We will examine each stage of financial development separately. This section will not describe the development of any one financial system but rather the 'logical historical order' of development of financial systems.

There are six major types of development that characterise the evolution of financial intermediation and the financial system. They can be classified according to the type of transactions that take place and the relevant financial claims that arise from these processes. They are:

1. barter,
2. commodity money,
3. fiat money,
4. primary securities,
5. equity securities,
6. financial intermediaries.

1. *Barter* – The first stage of development of the financial system is characterised by barter. The problem with barter, ie the exchange of goods for other goods, is that it requires a double coincidence of wants. For instance, if you have shoes and you

want to purchase socks then you have to find someone who has socks and wishes to purchase shoes. This is obviously not a very efficient means of exchange. Another problem with barter is that it does not allow for the storage of purchasing power. It is almost impossible to accumulate purchasing power under a barter economy because borrowing would be restricted and expenditure is therefore limited by the share of income accruing to each individual.

2. *Commodity money* – To overcome the problems associated with barter commodity money was devised. That is, one or more commodities set aside for generalised purchasing power, i.e. a medium of exchange with intrinsic value such as gold, silver, precious stones and other metals. Under such a system savings could be accumulated much more readily.

3. *Fiat money* – Before this next major stage of financial development occurred, steps were taken to overcome the constraints imposed by the commodity money economy. Among business units, partnerships were formed in order to pool accumulated savings. However, it was governments that provided the main impetus to the accumulation of individuals savings on a national scale, through taxation. Taxation was itself made easier by the creation and issue of legal tender money, sometimes called 'fiat money'. This could be obtained only by swapping commodity money, and symbolised the next stage of development of the financial system.

4. *Primary securities* – The next stage in the development of the financial system was indeed a logical one – the introduction of borrowing. For the first time deficit financing became available. Economic units were no longer restricted in their budgeting decisions to the amount of income accruing to them. They could now issue what are known as primary securities, i.e. promissory notes or IOUs in the form of bonds, mortgages or loans. Surplus units could now be offered a monetary inducement (interest) on the security or loan. With the development of primary securities came the corresponding development of markets where these securities could be traded. Again it was governments who encouraged the development of markets by issuing their own primary securities in large amounts. The development of markets increased the liquidity of these claims. Nevertheless, even at

this stage of development funds could only be raised by means of debt which, of course, has to finally be repaid.

5. *Equity securities* – The next stage of evolution came when it was discovered that the administration of businesses could be divorced from their ownership through the development of equity securities. With this the risk bearing function is borne by the equity (or share) owners rather than the management. The shareholders, through the process of incorporation, could become owners of the business with only limited liability. Surplus units could now in fact reduce risk further by holding a diversified portfolio of shares so reducing the risk that individual share fluctuations might adversely affect their profits.

The process so far consisted of deficit units issuing claims which are less risky and more convenient to surplus units than outright ownership and management of business assets. Revell (1975) notes that the need of businesses for the use of financial resources over a relatively long period of time set a constraint on equity security methods of financing. Each surplus unit needed a large part of its portfolio of financial assets in a form that ensured ready access to money balances in case of unforseen circumstances, etc. Wealthy surplus units could have relatively high proportions of their assets in non-money form, but less wealthy ones could not venture beyond money balances. In order to increase the total amount of debt financing it was necessary to meet the needs of the less wealthy surplus units for liquidity while providing the longer-term finance that business needed. These divergent needs could be reconciled only by the growth of specialised banks, which issued relatively risk-free, convenient and liquid claims to surplus units, and acquired primary securities from deficit units. These specialised bodies, as you should realise, are known as financial intermediaries.

6. *Financial intermediaries* – We have already discussed the financial intermediation process in this chapter. Figure 3.3 illustrates the main features and makes the distinction between primary and secondary securities.

Figure 3.3   *Primary and Secondary Securities*

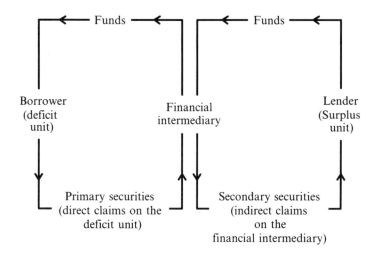

The securities which financial intermediaries issue are termed 'indirect claims' or secondary claims. As has already been stated elsewhere in this section, financial intermediaries can take the primary securities of deficit units and issue secondary securities in a form more attractive to surplus units as they will be less risky, more convenient and often more liquid than primary securities. They are able to do this because of the economies of scale that financial intermediaries enjoy on secondary securities. It is important to remember that primary securities are the same as direct claims whereas secondary securities are the same as indirect claims.

The one element which characterises every stage of development of the financial system is that of financial innovation. Each stage then is the result of innovation on the previous era. Financial innovation is a dynamic process that leads to continuous change in the development of financial systems. Rybczynski (1985) argues that as the financial system evolves, its ability to assume and carry risk increases. By improving the risk-assuming and risk-bearing capacity of an economy the evolution of the financial system helps to increase capital formation, savings and economic growth; this in turn assists the further transformation of the financial system, raising again risk bearing ability, investment and savings – and so on in a virtuous circle of advance. The virtuous circle of increasing capacity for risk associated with growing market orientation can be compared with the benefits of the division of labour and specialisation in the production of goods and services. This process reflects on the one hand growing financial intermediation and the acquisition of greater skills in risk selection; and on the other the emergence of new financial instruments for ultimate savers.

The regulatory framework also has a significant bearing on financial development in the sense that it can retard the speed of development, or it can assist it. If the regulatory framework helps the evolution of the financial system it will enhance its ability and willingness to take risk, if it retards its evolution it is likely to limit the extent of risk taking. The regulatory framework can delay the evolution of the financial system by imposing obstacles to charging market prices (i.e. by imposing limits on interest paid by institutions, so limiting the rate of return earned on savings, and probably, dividends paid on ordinary shares). Regulations may also restrict financial innovation by restricting the development of new financial instruments and methods of finance. A regulatory framework favourable to the evolution of the financial system would favour financial innovation, competition for savings and the development of new financial activities. Finally, it must be noted that possibly one of the main limitations to financial development may actually be the very institutional structures of our banks and other financial institutions. Powerful pressure groups may not wish to upset the status quo.

References and further reading

Goacher, David J. (1986) *An Introduction to Monetary Economics* (London: Financial Training).
Peasnell, K.V. and Ward, C.W.R. (1985) *British Financial Markets and Institutions* (London: Prentice Hall).
Revell, J.R.S. (1975) *The British Financial System* (London: Macmillan).
Rybczynski, T. (1985) 'Financial systems and public policy', *Royal Bank of Scotland Review*, December, pp. 35–45.
Wilson, Kevin W. (1983) *British Financial Institutions* (London: Pitman).

CHAPTER 4

THE CLASSIFICATION OF FINANCIAL INSTITUTIONS

INTRODUCTION

This chapter examines the problems associated with classifying financial institutions. Legislative distinctions made between commercial and investment banking, say in Japan and the United States, are not so relevant in the United Kingdom, or for that matter in other European countries. For example, Article 65 of the Japanese Securities and Exchange Law 1948 states that no bank, given a few exceptions, may undertake securities business. Similarly the US Glass-Steagall Act of 1933 also legally separates commercial and investment banking business. This distinction is hardly apparent in Europe where banks are generally classified according to their legal corporate status, that is whether they are private joint-stock institutions, mutual bodies (like building societies and co-operatives) or government owned. One must remember that with any classification system there are usually exceptions to the rule and this chapter aims to highlight some of these problems.

WAYS OF CLASSIFYING FINANCIAL INSTITUTIONS

There is nothing definitionally unique about a financial inter-mediary. Most economic units fulfil this role at one time or another. For instance if I was to take £100 out of my pocket and give you each £2 with which to buy some food, I would be acting as a financial intermediary. A more practical example of a financial intermediary would be where an industrial company extends credit to its debtors because of a delay in settling their debts with the company. A more extreme example of financial intermediation which by-passes the banking system is securitisation. Securitisation, quite simply, is the process by which firms issue securities in the capital markets in order to raise funds. These securities are purchased (mainly) by other companies. This process highlights the fact that deficit units are able to choose between obtaining direct funds from the capital market or indirect funds from the banking system. Direct finance increases when, for one reason or another, bank lending is restrictive. This process of direct borrowing where the banking system is by-passed is known as disintermediation. The largest financial intermediary of the United Kingdom is the government. The government acts as a financial intermediary by raising through its own borrowing nearly all the external finance required by public corporations and a large part of that needed by local authorities, and then making loans to these bodies. Obviously, then, a financial intermediary is very hard to categorise. There are many types. For our purpose we shall stick to financial institutions which perform this role.

Probably the easiest way to classify financial institutions is according to the nature of the claims which they issue, by their liabilities in other words. (This is because financial institutions tend to be more specialised on the liabilities side of the balance sheet.) The following classification comes from Revell (1975):

1. deposit institutions,
2. insurance and provident institutions,
3. portfolio institutions,
4. special investment agencies.

1. *Deposit institutions* – may be classified into two types; banks and other deposit institutions or 'near-banks'. You will see later on that the distinction is made because there are effectively two banking systems in operation in the United Kingdom. These are the deposit banking system and the wholesale banking system. Revell refers to the latter as the secondary banking system.

The deposit banks operate the payments system, that is they dominate the money transmission mechanism through the provision of chequing and other transaction facilities. The main players in this system are the London and Scottish clearing banks, the Northern Ireland banks, Girobank (formerly known as the National Giro) and the Trustee Savings Bank. Note that institutions other than banks offer chequing facilities, e.g. building societies.

Secondary banks perform a different function. Almost all of their customers are large corporations from whom they take deposits and to whom they extend credit. They are known as wholesale banking institutions. A chequing function is generally not a part of their service. They deal in the wholesale money markets and therefore carry a relatively small number of very large deposits, known as wholesale deposits. Secondary banks tend to have only a few branches. This contrasts with the deposit banks which carry a large number of small retail deposits in a nationwide branching system. The secondary banks include the Accepting houses (i.e. top rank merchant banks), other merchant banks, overseas banks and other banks included in the official statistics.

This classification is not so clear as it first suggests. Although the large London and Scottish clearing banks, e.g. National Westminster, Barclays, Lloyds, Midland, Royal Bank of Scotland, etc, have extensive branch networks that take retail deposits and provide the retail customers with a comprehensive range of banking services, they are also in the business of dealing with large corporations and operate in the wholesale money markets. The distinction is that secondary banks rely almost entirely on the latter type of business.

'Other deposit institutions' includes finance houses, savings banks, and building societies. These are included under this category because, like banks, they issue short-term claims, withdrawable on demand, i.e. short-term deposits. Finance houses are included in this category because, although they issue some claims which are not deposits, they perform much the same functions as the secondary banks, except they deal in considerably smaller amounts. They could be regarded as 'retail secondary banks'.

Revell (1975) also classifies three groups of financial institutions under the headings of insurance and provident institutions, portfolio institutions and special investment agencies, they are distinguishable by the nature of the secondary claims which they issue.

2. *Insurance and provident institutions* – the claims which these institutions issue have their values determined by actuarial calculations based on mortality statistics and expected future

interest rates. Such policies are known as life assurance
policies. Many of these companies, however, also do general
insurance business such as motor and fire insurance.

3. *Portfolio institutions* – are particular in the sense that the
secondary claims which they issue are essentially the same as
the direct claims which they hold. Institutions such as
investment trust companies and unit trusts (known as
mutual funds in the United States and Europe) build up
portfolios of shares and securities, mainly equity in the
United Kingdom (and government bonds in Europe), and
then issue their own shares and debentures, or units in the
case of unit trusts, in order to provide finance for their
activities. They provide the holders of their claims with
management advice and a share in a large diversified
portfolio which reduces risk below that which could be
achieved if the claim holders build up their own smaller
portfolios.

4. *Special investment agencies* – this is quite a small category in
the United Kingdom. This group would consist of financial
institutions which raise money on the capital markets in order
to make loans to, or purchase the shares of, other companies:
they are 'special' in so far as they specialise in lending to a
particular sector of industry. Examples of such institutions
would include, the 3is, Investors in Industry, which provides
venture capital for new businesses (this institution is majority
owned by the main UK clearing banks).

So far, one can see that we have classified financial
institutions solely according to the nature of the secondary
claims which they issue. There are, however, many other ways
to classify financial institutions. Distinctions can be made
between:

1. private and public financial institutions,
2. retail and wholesale financial institutions,
3. first degree and second degree financial intermediaries.

Private and public institutions – among the private financial
institutions, two further distinctions become apparent. The
first is between unincorporated and incorporated bodies, and
the second is between mutual and proprietary bodies. If a
company of any sort is incorporated it means it is a body

corporate in law. A building society, for example, is an incorporated business, i.e. it is a body corporate but it cannot issue equity. Corporate status is achieved usually by registration under the 1985 Companies Act. Conversely, an unincorporated firm is one that is not a body corporate in law. All proprietary bodies are incorporated. Mutual bodies may be either incorporated or unincorporated. Either way, they consist solely of their members with no outside holdings in the company. As there are no outside shareholders then all profits are either retained as reserves for the company or distributed to the members as bonuses. The mutual form of organisation is quite common in life assurance, where the bodies are usually called 'societies' to distinguish them from the proprietory companies. Probably the most common example of mutual societies, however, are the building societies, which are incorporated under the Building Societies Act, but act as mutual societies. The 1986 Building Societies Act, which came into force in January 1987, has enabled building societies to become incorporated public limited companies like the banks. Public limited companies are those that are large enough to fulfil the International Stock Exchange of the United Kingdom and the Republic of Ireland (previously known as the London Stock Exchange) requirements for a full listing on the exchange. They, therefore, tend to have a large number of shareholders and find it relatively easy to raise funds through the capital market. Most of the large companies, whether financial or not, have public limited status, e.g. National Westminster Bank plc (public limited company).

Retail and wholesale financial institutions – this distinction has already been mentioned earlier on in this chapter. Retail financial institutions tend to deal with large numbers of small deposits/loans consumer business whereas wholesale institutions deal with a few large accounts. The distinction, however, is often arbitrary as a basis for classifying institutions since many institutions operate in both markets.

First degree and second degree financial intermediaries – first degree intermediaries are institutions that receive the majority of their funds from non-financial intermediaries. Second degree intermediaries can be described as those which perform only second degree functions, in the sense that they receive all their funds from other financial institutions. The only financial institutions which accurately fit this description, however, are probably reinsurance companies. Many institutions act partially as second degree intermediaries. A classic example would be the discount houses. The main function of the discount houses is to act as specialised banks enabling other banks to adjust their liquidity.

What is a bank?

The definition of what constitutes a bank differs in every country and it should be made clear at this point that the following definition applies solely to the United Kingdom. It was not until the UK Banking Act of 1979 that a system of legal definitions for banks was laid down. Before that time, only listed banks, i.e. those submitting returns to the Bank of England, were recognised as having banking status. However, it was often the case that certain institutions which called themselves banks in fact operated outside the direct sphere of influence of the Bank of England. The 1979 Banking Act made a distinction between what were called recognised banks and licensed deposit-takers. Essentially the 1979 Act sought to bring the United Kingdom into line with the European Community's directive on credit institutions. The criteria which the Bank of England adopted to determine a recognised bank was determined by Schedule 2 of the Act. The following factors were taken into account:

1. a good reputation must exist for the deposit-taking institution,
2. a wide range of banking services, specialist or otherwise must be provided such as:

   (a) current and deposit account facilities or accepting funds in the wholesale market,
   (b) provision of loans and overdrafts, or lending in the wholesale money markets,
   (c) foreign exchange facilities,
   (d) the handling of bills of exchange and promissory notes including financing foreign trade,

(e) financial advice and the provision of facilities for the purchase and sale of investments,

3. a minimum amount of capital and reserves.

Those institutions not recognised as banks, but licensed to accept deposits from the public (licensed deposit takers) had to similarly fulfil criteria on minimum capital and reserves, adequate liquidity and solvency and on the quality of their management. The distinction between recognised banks and licensed deposit takers has recently ended since the passing of the Banking Act 1987. All deposit institutions now have to fulfil the same criteria if they wish to achieve bank status.

Different types of UK financial institutions

The various types of UK financial institutions are set out below:

1. *The banking sector*
   (a) the Banking Department of the Bank of England,
   (b) the deposit banks – the London clearing banks; the Scottish clearing banks; the Northern Ireland banks; other deposit banks,
   (c) the secondary banks – merchant, overseas, foreign and consortium banks,
   (d) the discount houses and brokers,
   (e) Girobank (formerly known as National Giro).

2. *Other financial intermediaries*
   (a) other deposit institutions – building societies; the finance houses and National Savings Bank,
   (b) insurance and provident institutions – the insurance companies; the pension funds,
   (c) portfolio institutions – unit trusts; investment trusts.

Reference and further reading

Revell, J.R.S. (1975) *The British Financial System* (London: Macmillan).

CHAPTER 5

THE CONCEPT OF MONEY AND HOW BANKS CREATE DEPOSITS

INTRODUCTION

The first part of this chapter examines the problems associated with defining money and also lists its main functions and attributes. The second part describes how banks are able to create deposits through the credit multiplier process.

THE CONCEPT OF MONEY

This section will deal with five main questions:

1. What is money?
2. What functions does it perform?
3. What are the necessary attributes of money?
4. How can we measure money?
5. Why do people/economic units hold money?

What is money?

In general money is represented by the coins and notes which we use in our daily lives; it is the commodity readily acceptable by all people wishing to undertake transactions. It is also a means of expressing a value for any kind of article or service. Goods and services are valued in monetary terms so we can easily compare one article or service to another entirely different article or service. Additionally, we know from the monetary price how much is required in order to obtain any particular article or service. However, as noted earlier, we did not always have money in our society. Primitive societies existed through barter or direct exchange of goods. The drawbacks of this type of system have already been pointed out. What was needed was a medium of exchange on which all parties could agree and which would be used to express the relative prices of each of the goods which were to be exchanged. Once society accomplished this, money was created.

What function does money perform?

Medium of exchange is probably the main function of money. If barter were the only type of trade possible, there would be many situations in which people would not be able to obtain the goods and services that they wanted most. The advantage of the use of money is that it provides the owner with generalised purchasing power. The use of money gives the owner flexibility over the type and quantities of goods he buys, the time and place of his purchases, and the parties with whom he chooses to deal. A critical characteristic of a medium of exchange is that it be acceptable as such. It must be readily exchangeable for other things. It is usual for the government to designate certain coins or paper currency as the medium of exchange.

If money is acceptable as a medium of exchange it almost certainly comes to act as a unit of account by which the prices of all commodities can be defined and then compared. This, of course, simplifies the task of deciding how we wish to divide our income between widely disparate items. For this reason it is sometimes said that money acts as a measure of value, and this is true both if value is taken to mean both 'price' and 'worth', the latter being a much more subjective concept.

Money is also a liquid store of value in that it provides individuals with a means of holding and accumulating their wealth in a form which can, at any time, be converted immediately into goods and services. When a person holds money as a store of value he/she is effectively treating it as a substitute to holding alternative forms of financial assets such as bonds or deposit accounts. The holder of money therefore foregoes the payment of an explicit yield in return for the acceptance of an implicit yield in the form of convenience and certainty.

Money can also act as a standard of deferred payment. Due to this function it is possible to undertake a number of transactions in the present and actually settle the account (or bill) at some time in the future, e.g. buy now and pay later. The sale and production of goods is made easier by money performing this function since goods can be provided through trade credit, labour and raw materials can be obtained by the producer, and the various parties will know the sums involved and payments to be made at a future date. Although this particular function of money is not essential for lending, borrowing and production to take place, it certainly makes such activities easier. Money's function as a standard for deferred payment may be questioned in times of high inflation where the real value of money declines rapidly. In such situations the debtor would benefit from a deferred payment. The main point to make here, then, as concerns 'the function of money as a standard for deferred payment' is that it permits commercial lending to take place. A borrower can agree that if a lender supplies him with ten units of money today, he/she will pay back eleven units in (say) three months time. The charging of interest has become possible.

What are the necessary attributes of money?

The acceptability of a particular item as money is the first prerequisite for its use. Every individual using the money must be sure that all other people within the area or country will accept and use the money in just the same way. Many types of commodity can take on the role of money if it is widely accepted. During the Second World War, for example, many people lost faith in paper money and they began to substitute chocolate, cigarettes, petrol, etc., for money.

As well as being acceptable money must be uniform, it must be homogenous. There must be no advantage in holding particular types of money in preference to others. Each unit of currency should be interchangeable with each similar unit. If this can be achieved, people will not care which particular unit of currency they accept in payment of a debt, but will take any, provided that it is of the correct face value. This attribute is sometimes called 'fungibility'. The fact that money must be homogenous is born out in what is known as Gresham's law which states that bad money drives out good.

Money must also be divisible into smaller units, and in so doing, these smaller units must not lose value when compared to larger units. For example, two 50 pence pieces are equal to £1 just as 10 ten pence pieces are equal to £1. A problem experienced when using items of intrinsic value as money is that their division into smaller units can reduce the value of the components to much less than their value as a complete whole, e.g. some Iron Age societies are believed to have used axe heads as currency. Part of their value derived from their usefulness as potential tools; broken up into smaller pieces of metal, this utility was lost and their value reduced accordingly.

As well as being divisible, the units of money must be stable over long periods of time. Pounds and pence, dollars and cents must all convey the same meaning in the future as they do now. This does not mean that the buying power or purchasing power of money should stay the same, but rather that £100 saved now will still be £100 in two, five or ten years. In terms of buying or purchasing power, inflation is likely to erode buying power over time.

Money is also expected to be durable. The durability of money has an effect on its stability of value where an item of intrinsic value is used. If the commodity is likely to wear away with use or deteriorate with age, it will naturally lose purchasing power. Paper money tends to be outlived by metallic money. This, of course, was the reason for the introduction of the £1 coin in the United Kingdom in 1983.

Finally money should be recognisable, no special skills or intelligence must be required in order to understand how to identify and use the money. In addition it should also be portable. Money must have a high value in relation to its size so that it can be easily carried about in sufficiently large amounts for everyday trading.

Any item which can fulfil the above qualities has the possibility of being used as money. In most cases it is the first quality, acceptability, which is of paramount importance.

How can we measure money?

You will remember from the previous sections in this chapter that the opportunity cost of holding money as a store of value is the interest foregone on holding higher yielding forms of financial assets. For example, if you save £100 in cash under your bed for a year then you forego the interest you would have earned if the £100 had been put in a building society at the beginning of the year. To say that there is an opportunity cost to holding money as a store of value implies that money is substitutable for other goods. But just how substitutable is it? Although money possesses a unique property as a final means of payment, it is not unique as a financial asset since there are obviously many other forms of financial asset available.

Let us suppose we have four assets; cash, current account deposits (sometimes known as chequing accounts), deposit accounts and building society deposits. Furthermore, we will assume that the rate of interest paid on building society deposits rises substantially and the rate of interest on deposit accounts does not alter. What is likely to happen? Well, first of all people will probably decide to switch from deposit accounts to building society accounts, implying a certain degree of substitutability. If then, suppose that the rate on deposit accounts rises then we may expect to see a certain amount of switching back from building society accounts to deposit accounts. But what would be the effect on the size of the current accounts? It may well be that individuals decide to reduce their current accounts to the very minimum required, or they may adjust the timing of their spending so that they are able to reduce their current accounts and transfer funds to deposit accounts. This type of response by individuals to changes in interest rates, if it did occur in the way we have suggested, could be an indication that the four types of asset are in some degree substitutes. If the response to changes in interest rates is relatively large, ie a small change in interest rates results in a large switch in the holding of one form of asset for another, this indicates a high degree of substitutability between the assets. If a large change in interest rates produced only a small change in the holding of one form of asset, then this would suggest a low degree of substitutability. (Note: the degree of substitutability can be measured by using price elasticity of demand and cross elasticity of demand concepts from economic theory.)

There is evidence that substitutability does exist between various types of deposit and it has been suggested, therefore, that attempting to identify definitely those assets which are unambiguously 'money' is a mistaken approach. Nevertheless, one can accept the implications of the 'substitutability' arguments and, in fact, the monetary authorities utilise narrow money and broad money definitions for monetary policy purposes. Figures 5.1 and 5.2 show how the authorities measure the money supply. Note that the authorities have regularly (and sometimes mysteriously?)

Figure 5.1 *Relationships Among the Monetary and Liquidity Aggregates and Their Components Prior to May 1987*

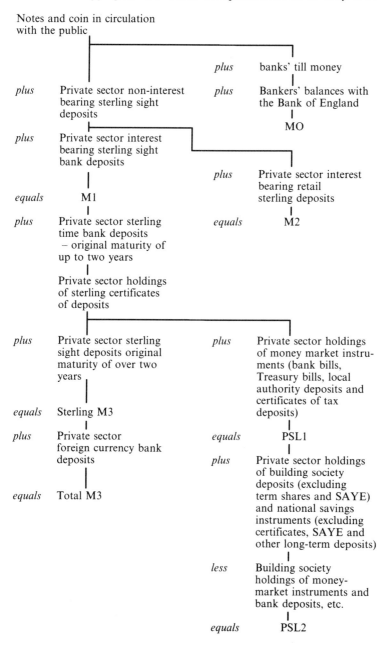

Figure 5.2 *Relationships Among Monetary Aggregates and Their Components after May 1987*

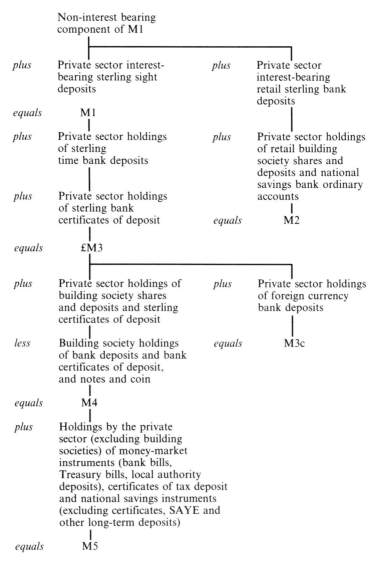

Non-interest bearing
component of M1

plus   Private sector interest-   *plus*   Private sector
bearing sterling sight   interest-bearing
deposits   retail sterling bank
deposits

equals   M1

plus   Private sector holdings   *plus*   Private sector holdings
of sterling   of retail building
time bank deposits   society shares and
deposits and national
savings bank ordinary

plus   Private sector holdings   accounts
of sterling bank
certificates of deposit   *equals*   M2

equals   £M3

plus   Private sector holdings of   *plus*   Private sector holdings
building society shares   of foreign currency
and deposits and sterling   bank deposits
certificates of deposit

less   Building society holdings   *equals*   M3c
of bank deposits and bank
certificates of deposit,
and notes and coin

equals   M4

plus   Holdings by the private
sector (excluding building
societies) of money-market
instruments (bank bills,
Treasury bills, local authority
deposits), certificates of tax deposit
and national savings instruments
(excluding certificates, SAYE and
other long-term deposits)

equals   M5

Notes: M0 is still defined as in Figure 5.1
Source: *Bank of England Quarterly Bulletin,* May 1987

changed the different measures of the money supply. There are now seven specific UK money measures, M_o, M_1, M_2, £M_3, M_{3c}, M_4 and M_5. M_o is the narrowest measure whereas M_5 is the broadest (see Figures 5.1 and 5.2 for the relevant definitions). Figure 5.1 shows the different measurements of money M_o, M_1, etc. (known as money aggregates) before May 1987. In May 1987 certain definitions changed and these are shown in Figure 5.2.

Why do people/economic units hold money?

John Maynard Keynes introduced a threefold classification for holding money. They are the transactions, precautionary and speculative motives.

Transactions motive – the transactions motive results in the use of money as a medium of exchange. People need money to handle ordinary transactions and are seriously inconvenienced if they do not have money available. The amount of money needed for transactions depends in part on the volume of the purchases made. In addition, the frequency of income received makes a difference to the transactions demand. The more frequent the payments, the smaller the average cash balance that must be on hand to finance transactions. Regularity of payments is also important.

Precautionary motive – the precautionary motive for holding money is related to the liquidity of money and the use of money as a store of value. When prices are stable, money gives people a type of protection as insurance does, against some types of risk. Business firms also have many needs for liquidity.

Speculative motives – money is also held because it provides people with the liquidity needed to shift readily to other assets. This is referred to as the speculative motive for holding money because it involves outguessing movements in the prices of securities or goods. If individuals expect the prices of goods to fall, they may build up their money balances so as to take advantage of the lower prices in the future. If people expect interest rates to rise (and bond prices to fall), they will tend to build up their money balances so as to be in a position to purchase bonds when their prices reach rock bottom. On the other hand, if they expect interest rates to fall (and bond prices to rise), the speculative demand for money will be relatively small.

The credit multiplier or how banks create deposits

One of the oldest topics of discussion in banking theory is the power of the banks to 'create' deposits. Bankers have usually held that such creation was impossible as they could only lend after receiving a fresh deposit. Economists have insisted, however, that deposit liabilities could be manufactured by the banking system. The basis for this alleged power on behalf of banks, to create deposits, stems from the fact that bank deposits are generally accepted as money by the public. The public is confident that bank deposits can always be converted for cash; current account deposits can be converted on demand. However, not everyone will want all their money back on any particular day. As a result of this fact, banks do not have to keep all the money deposited with them, they only need to hold a small amount which is likely to be needed each day. Because this is so, it is essential to maintain public confidence in the banking system. In recent times the maintenance of confidence has depended on the adherence of banks to certain legal ratios concerning the liquidity of its assets, in particular, to a specified ratio of cash to deposits.

Table 5.1 illustrates this point and shows the simplest version of what has come to be known as the credit multiplier. (a) represents the position of the bank's balance sheet before disturbance; (b) represents the position immediately after disturbance; and (c) represents the point at which equilibrium is restored.

Table 5.1 *The Case of a Single Bank Under a 10 Per Cent Cash Ratio (£ million)*

	a	b	c
Liabilities			
deposits	50000	50050	50050
Assets			
cash	5000 (10%)	5050 (10.1%)	5005 (10%)
advances	45000	45000	45045

In *position (a)* we assume that the bank has £50 000 million worth of deposits and is adhering to a 10 per cent cash ratio. That is, for every £10 it receives in deposits it must keep £1 in cash and can advance the other £9 as loans. In this case the bank's £50 000 million worth of deposits are broken down into £5 000 million cash and £45 000 million loans.

Position (b) shows the immediate effect of an increase in £50 million of deposits on the simplified bank balance sheet. This £50 million of deposits goes immediately into cash. The cash ratio has, therefore, increased from 10 per cent to 10.1 per cent. As the bank earns no money by simply holding excess cash, it will wish to reduce this ratio back to 10 per cent, which is the minimum requirement.

Position (c) to return back to the initial 10 per cent cash ratio, the bank will increase its advances (or loans) by £45 million, by correspondingly reducing its cash balance by the same amount.

In this simplified example, then, the credit multiplier, defined as the ratio of change in deposits to the change in level of cash, is:

$$\text{Credit multiplier} = \frac{\text{Change in the level of deposits}}{\text{Change in the level of cash}}$$

$$\frac{50050 - 50000}{5005 - 5000} = \frac{50}{5} = 10$$

You should note that this is the same as the reciprocal of the cash ratio.

Here, then, it should be clear that this individual bank has not created any deposits, but merely lent out a proportion of its deposits as advances. Indeed, if a banking system consisted of only one bank, it would be fairly easy to accept that it would soon learn the simple arithmetic relating an increase in cash to the additional deposits which that cash could support, and that it would proceed straight from position (b) to position (c). Most banking systems, however, consist of many banks, each operating on its own and for its own profit. As such, when one bank makes a loan, we can expect this loan to end up with another bank as a deposit.

Table 5.2 illustrates the features of credit creation where there is more than one bank. In Table 5.2 we assume that each of the four banks begins with £5000 million worth of deposits. We assume also that the 10 per cent cash ratio still exists. In this example, Bank A receives £50 million of deposits and it retains £5 million cash and lends out the other £45 million. As its customers draw cheques on its advances, we can assume that they are all paid into accounts with a second bank, Bank B, which will in turn receive £45 million of deposits. This second bank will behave in exactly the same way as the first one; it will retain £4.5 million in cash and lend out £40.5 million (90 per cent of £45 million). The £40.5 million now becomes a gain of deposits for the third bank, Bank C, and so on down the line. Table 5.2 shows the position for the first four banks in the sequence. For these first four steps in the sequence, the original £50 million of cash has generated an additional £126.95 million of deposits (£50 million + £45 million and £40.5 million + £36.45 million), and the same process will continue for many more stages.

Table 5.2   *The Banking System Under a 10 Per Cent Cash Ratio*
              (£ million)

	Bank A	*Bank B*	*Bank C*	*Bank D*
Liabilities				
deposits	5050	5045	5040.5	5036.45
Assets				
cash	505	500.0	504.05	503.645
advances	4545	4540.5	4536.45	4532.605

At each stage the growth in deposits is exactly 90 per cent of what it was at the previous stage. (This is because the cash ratio is 10 per cent.) From this it should be obvious that here we are dealing with an convergent geometrical series. The sum of the additional deposits created is as follows:

$$50 + 45 + 40.5 + 36.45 + 32.605 + \ldots$$

This can be also represented as:

$$50 + (50 \times 0.9) + (50 \times 0.9^2) + (50 \times 0.9^3) + (50 \times 0.9^4) + \ldots$$

This series will sum to $50/(1-0.9) = 500$

Put simply:

$$\text{Credit multiplier} = \frac{1}{\text{cash ratio}} = \frac{1}{0.1} = 10$$

As the multiplier is 10, then with an injection of £50 million of cash, the process will end (achieve equilibrium) when an additional £500 million of deposits has been created.

As with most theory, the assumptions behind this simple model are not very realistic. Just as the original increments of cash and deposits are likely to accrue to several banks within the system, so the subsequent gains of cash and deposits are likely to be diffused throughout the system, some indeed coming straight back to the lending bank as the borrower makes a payment to another customer of the same bank. These considerations, however, do not deter from the logic of the process, which depends only on the supposition that each bank will behave identically in the process of adhering to its cash ratio. If any one bank took no action on receiving excess cash, the multiplier process would break down. For it to work smoothly, all banks must act together.

It should be apparent from this simple model that both the practical banker and the economist are right about the 'creating of deposits'. The practical banker is correct because each bank in turn has received additional cash and deposits before it has increased its lending, and they lend only 90 per cent of the amount received. However, the economist is also correct in stating that additional deposits have been 'created' because the original increment of £50 million has grown to an ultimate sum of £500 million.

The credit multiplier and leakages from the banking system

As we have already mentioned, the credit multiplier has a value equal to the reciprocal of the cash ratio, but in practice, various leakages occur and the actual multiplier is nowhere near the theoretical value as represented by the reciprocal of the cash ratio.

When banks acquire assets from their customers they can do so on the basis of 'created' deposits, but this possibility is not open for those assets which they acquire through the Bank of England; they must pay cash for them. Thus, whenever the clearing banks acquire assets through the Bank of England in the course of the multiplier process, there is a leakage, and the value of the multiplier is reduced accordingly. A classic example of such a leakage is the purchase of treasury bills. These leakages are referred to as internal because the transactions are initiated by the banks themselves. External leakages are those initiated by customers, and involve the clearing banks in the replenishment to their stocks of till money, because customers have withdrawn notes and coins.

In general, a leakage occurs when cash leaves and does not return to the banking system.

It is important to note that it is the nature of the transaction and not the particular kind of asset involved which causes a leakage. Thus banks can purchase government bonds from their customers without there being a leakage as long as that cash eventually returns to the banking system as a deposit. If, however, the bank purchases bonds directly from the government, this does represent a leakage as the cash actually leaves the banking system.

In the two examples illustrated above, in Tables 5.1 and 5.2, we have adhered to certain assumptions. They are:

1. That all banks work to some balance sheet ratios. In our examples so far it has been a 10 per cent cash ratio.
2. That all payments are trapped within the banking system.
3. That neither the public or banks have any desire to hold excess amounts of cash.

In the real world, however, none of the above assumptions hold. The 10 per cent cash ratio is quite unrealistic. Banks are much more likely to be concerned with their reserve assets ratio (sometimes called liquid assets ratio) which is comprised of cash and other relatively liquid assets. A more realistic cash ratio would probably be around say 1.5 per cent of total assets with liquid assets comprising at least 6 or 7 per cent of total assets. The credit multiplier is more likely to be determined (restricted) by the size of the reserve asset ratio and you would find that certain worked examples in various textbooks will use this ratio to explain the multiplier process. As we have already mentioned, cash may leave the banking system if banks purchase government debt, etc. and, therefore, leakages do occur. The larger the leakage, the smaller the size of the credit multiplier. In addition, the public and banks do hold excess amounts of cash mainly for precautionary reasons, and as a result, this will also reduce the size of the credit multiplier.

How useful and how relevant is the concept of the credit multiplier?

Well, like other concepts in the field of economics, the simple banking multiplier concept which we have outlined forces us to state our assumptions clearly and to follow through a process to the end. It has also enabled us to underline the basic distinction, which lies at the root of the banking mechanism, between transactions in which deposits remain trapped within the banking system, because they are between customers of the same group of banks, and transactions with outsiders, in which cash and deposits leak out of the banking system. To be of any practical value, however, the banking multiplier would have to be stable and predictable. It is, in reality, neither.

CHAPTER 6

MAJOR SERVICES PROVIDED BY UK DEPOSIT BANKS

INTRODUCTION

The deposit or retail banks dominate sterling denominated banking business in the United Kingdom. These banks either have extensive branch networks or participate directly in a UK clearing system. They include the London clearing banks (Barclays, Coutts, Lloyds, Midland and National Westminster), Scottish clearing banks (Bank of Scotland, Clydesdale and Royal Bank of Scotland), Northern Ireland Banks (Allied Irish, Bank of Ireland, Northern Bank and Ulster Bank), Trustee Savings Bank Group, Co-operative Bank, Yorkshire Bank and Girobank. As a group they are often referred to as the UK clearing banks. The following chapter examines the main features of UK payment clearing systems as well as the major services provided by these banks.

UK PAYMENT CLEARING SYSTEMS

A unique feature of the UK banking system, compared with other European countries, is that a few banks have traditionally dominated the payment system and these have been able to establish their own clearing houses to arrange payment and settlement procedures. A payment clearing system has existed in London for over 200 years and for the majority of that period it has been based in offices known as the Bankers' Clearing House. This institution was owned and controlled by the major retail banks through the Committee of London and Scottish Bankers (CLSB). Other banks have been allowed to join the operation; the Bank of England in 1864, Co-operative Bank and the Central Trustee

Savings Bank in 1975 and Girobank in 1983, but these did not share in the ownership or directly participate in the clearing operations. As a result of various reports which questioned the dominant role played by the CLSB, a working party was set up in March 1984, under the chairmanship of Denis Child, Director and Deputy Group Chief Executive of National Westminster Bank, to review the organisation, membership and control of the payment clearing systems in the United Kingdom. In December 1984 the Child Report was published and this recommended substantial changes to the organisation of the payment clearing systems as well as setting up a new structure and new rules for obtaining membership to the clearing system. The recommendations contained in the Child Report were accepted by the ten banks that controlled the Bankers Clearing House and were implemented by the end of 1985.

The UK payments clearing system since December 1985

At the top of the new system was an umbrella organisation that monitored the development of the operational clearings and of the payments industry as a whole. Beneath this 'umbrella' were three individual clearing companies, covering three types of clearings. The control and ownership of these companies was to be 'in the hands' of all member institutions participating in the clearing system. The umbrella organisation was set up in October 1985 and is known as the Association for Payment Clearing Services (APACS). The three clearing companies established in December 1985 were as follows:

1. *Cheque and Credit Clearing Company Limited* – this company is responsible for 'bulk paper clearings' of cheques and credits in England and Wales. Predominantly low-value, high-volume clearing business. Paper clearings in Scotland and Northern Ireland have not been included in the new structure.

2. *Clearing House Automated Payment System (CHAPS) and Town Clearing Company Limited* – this company is responsible for the clearing of high value cheques and credits (those exceeding £10 000) providing same-day settlements. That is the clearing and settlement process takes place on the same day, unlike small denomination cheques which take a minimum of two days to be cleared. The Town Clearing Services covers only high-value cheques

'drawn on and paid into members' branches within the designated town clearing area of the City of London'.

3. *BACS Limited* (formerly known as Bankers Automated Clearing Services Limited) – this provides an electronic bulk clearing service for direct debits, standing orders and other automated credit transfers. BACS in fact has been operating in some form or another since 1968.

During 1987 a fourth company was established, Eftpos UK Limited. This company aimed to deal with transactions that are to be cleared through a national electronic funds tranfer at the point of sale (EFTPOS) system when it is fully developed. This company shut down in February 1990 when individual banks stated that they would go it alone on Eftpos. The members of APACS and the various operational clearing systems are listed in Table 6.1.

Table 6.1 *Membership of APACS and the Operational Clearings, July 1987*

Members	APACS	Cheque and credit clearing	CHAPS and town clearing	BACS
Abbey National Building Society	x	–	–	x
Bank of England	x	x	x	x
Bank of Scotland	x	x	x	x
Barclays Bank	x	x	x	x
Citibank	x	–	x	–
Clydesdale Bank	x	–	x	x
Co-operative Bank	x	x	x	x
Coutts & Co.	x	–	x	x
Girobank	x	x	x	x
Halifax Building Society	x	–	–	x
Lloyds Bank	x	x	x	x
Midland Bank	x	x	x	x
National Westminster Bank	x	x	x	x
Royal Bank of Scotland	x	x	x	x
Standard Chartered Bank	x	–	x	–
TSB England and Wales	x	x	x	x
Yorkshire Bank	x	–	–	x
	17	10	14	15

Source: *Bank of England Quarterly Bulletin*, August 1987

Table 6.2 *Growth in Payments 1980–87*

Clearing[1]	Volume (million of items)			Value (£ billion)		
	1980	1987	Change (%)	1980	1987	Change (%)
Cheque	1454	2061	+42	406	860	+112
Credit	214	186	-13	52	92	+ 77
CHAPS[2]	–	4.4		–	7332	
Town	5	4.0	+6.8	4051	8325	286
BACS	438	1071	+145	91	356	+291

Notes: [1] Excludes inter-branch items
[2] CHAPS commenced operations on 9 February 1984
Source: *Abstract of Banking Statistics*, Statistical Unit, CLSB, May 1988

A significant feature of the payments system over the last decade has been the continued growth in both volumes and values of items cleared. Table 6.2 illustrates these changes. It shows the importance of BACS, 'the largest automated clearing system in the world' and also confirms the continued popularity of cheques in routine money transmission transactions. The average daily turnover in the CHAPS and Town Clearings in 1987 amounted to some £62 billion, compared with £16 billion for Town Clearing in 1980. Daily turnover for cheque clearings amounted to nearly £2.5 billion. Table 6.2 does not include figures for credit and charge card transactions. By the end of 1987 the CLSB estimates that over 750 million of such transactions took place with a value of turnover exceeding £24 billion. Cash advances on credits cards accounted for around ten per cent of this value. To put these fugures into perspective, however, APACS estimated in 1987 that the number of cash transations for values in excess of £5 is estimated to be around 4 billion per annum.

NON-CASH METHODS OF PAYMENT

Cheque payments

Cheques are the most common form of retail customer payment methods in the United Kingdom. If individual A purchases goods and gives a cheque to individual B, it is up to B to deposit the cheque in his own bank account. Individual B's bank then initiates the request to debit individual A's account. A's bank authorises (clears) the cheque and a transfer of assets (settlement) then takes place. Because of this procedure cheque payments are known as debit transfers because they are written requests to debit the payees account.

Giro payments

Giro payments are known as credit transfers because they are initiated by the payer making a request to their bank that a credit be made to another individual's account. These bank giro credits are cleared, as with cheques, through the Cheque and Credit Clearing Company or 'in-house' usually within three working days of the payment being made into a bank.

Standing orders

This is an instrument from the customer to the bank to pay a fixed sum, at regular intervals, into the account of another individual or company. The bank has the responsibility to remember to make the payments.

Direct debits

A direct debit is when the customer authorises his or her bank to debit his or her account at the instruction of a specified payee. These amounts can be either fixed or variable and the times at which debiting takes place can be either fixed or variable. For example, many retail customers pay their utility bills (electricity, gas, water rates, etc.) in this way.

Plastic cards

Plastic cards include credit cards, debit cards, cheque guarantee cards, travel and entertainment cards and 'Smart' or 'Memory' cards. Technically, plastic cards do not act themselves as a payment mechanism; they help to identify the customers and assist in creating either a paper or electronic payment. The number of these cards, especially credit cards, has grown dramatically over the last decade.

Credit cards – these provide their holders with a pre-arranged credit limit to use at retailers which have agreed to pay the credit card company a set commission on the balance. Credit cards can also be used to obtain cash advances through automated teller machines. Credit is interest free if it is paid off before a certain date, but if the full balance is not cleared it attracts interest. Visa and Mastercard are the two most important bank-owned credit card organisations and their total UK card issue amounted to 25.7 million by the end of 1988.

Debit cards – these are issued directly by the banks and allow customers to withdraw money from their bank accounts. They can also be used to obtain account information and such like when used through automated teller machines (ATMs).

Cheque guarantee cards – these were first introduced in the United Kingdom during the 1960s in an attempt by banks to attract more retail customers. During this period banks' efforts to attract more retail customers had been heavily restricted by retailers reluctance to accept cheques. By the mid-1980s there were approximately 22 million guarantee cards in the United Kingdom issued free. Some cheque guarantee cards can also act as debit cards.

Travel and entertainment cards – these cards are issued to high net-worth (rich) individuals to provide exclusive payments facilities. They have no credit limits but balances must be cleared at the end of every month, although some, such as Mastercards Gold card and American Expresses Platinum card do offer longer-term credit facilities. The holder has to pay a fixed annual sum for the use of such a card. The financial qualifications for cardholders are more stringent than for 'everyday' credit cards, and qualifications become more onerous as one steps up the plastic card hierarchy. The leader in this field is American Express which currently offers the Green, Gold and the most exclusive, Platinum, card.

'Smart', memory or chip cards – over the last decade or so there has been substantial developments in micro-chip technology attached to plastic cards. These cards can carry out more sophisticated transactions than conventional plastic cards. They come in two forms, simple cards capable of storing units of value and more advanced cards which have microprocessor capabilities. The former

are in widespread use in the United Kingdom especially for operating public telephones. The latter are currently at an experimental stage and are not widely used in the United Kingdom, or other European countries for that matter.

Electronic funds transfer

Offering an efficient payment system is an expensive business. It is also a volume business. Automating the processing of payments has given banks genuine economies of scale and scope. Developments in cheque encoding, transactions and automated debits and credit transfers bears testimony to this. The general move towards electronic banking can be identified if one views the alternative networks of electronic terminals that provide banks with various ways of electronic processing and transmission of information. Systems can be distinguished according to the location of the payments machinery. The different networks include:

1. automated Clearing Houses,
2. automated Branch Counter Terminals,
3. proprietary or shared ATM networks,
4. EFTPOS terminals (Electronic Funds Transfer at Point of Sale),
5. Home and Office banking terminals (HOB terminals).

As already mentioned the automated clearing houses in the United Kingdom include the Bankers Automated Clearing Service (BACS) and the Clearing House Automated Payments System (CHAPS). The former transacts many bank giro, standing order and direct debit transfers. The latter may be used for making payments to be completed within the same working day, sometimes known as same day settlement.

Automated branch counter terminals are mainly found in building societies, although some deposit banks have limited facilities for payments purposes. Deposit banks in Europe make wider use of these terminals.

New technology has helped to free the retail customer from having to go into the bank. The growth in automated teller machines (ATMs) over the last two decades has illustrated this point. The most sophisticated of these machines enables the consumer to withdraw cash from a range of accounts, make deposits, enquire about balances, make transfers and pay bills, order cheque books and issue statement printouts. These services are being continually extended. For example, in November 1986, the UK Trustee Savings Bank Group installed in two of its branches ATMs which offer advice on insurance services. As banks find they can offer a broad range of products and access new locations through this automated facility, the need for a comprehensive branch network of the traditional kind becomes less necessary.

Electronic funds transfer at the point of sale (EFTPOS) and Home and Office Banking (HOB) systems are less operationalised than ATM networks. The majority of experiments and systems being tried for EFTPOS involve connecting a retailer's cash register so that electronic messages can be transmitted to the bank. The customer's account is automatically debited and the retailer's credited. As a result, there is no need for any paper transaction. Developments in EFTPOS have led to talk of the coming of the cashless society. Midland Bank has become the first major clearing bank in Britain to launch a full-scale experiment in electronic shopping. The project, called Speedline, involves the installation of 30 Nixdorf EFTPOS terminals in shops, chain stores and petrol stations in Northampton. Clydesdale Bank runs a similar system called Counterplus in Scotland.

A potential future development in the provision of bank services is known as Home and Office Banking Systems (HOBS) which completely frees customers from the branch networks. Cash management services, balance enquiries, funds transfers, bill payment and the like can be initiated with the use of a TV screen, personal computer or variable tone, push-button telephone, depending on the system available. At the present time, France leads the world in home banking. The French post and telephone service has given out over 1.5 million Minitel videotex terminals free. Crédit Commercial de France already has 75 000 home banking systems. In the United Kingdom, various systems have already become operational including those of the Nottingham Building Society, Bank of Scotland, Nationwide Anglia and the Halifax Building Society.

DEPOSIT AND LENDING FACILITIES

Deposits

Deposit-taking is still the most important factor in maintaining an established customer base. As customers become more financially sophisticated, they demand better facilities from their bank account. In general, customers want four things from their accounts: early and quick access to money, increased credit availability when necessary, money working for them at all times and reliable information about their financial position. Retail customers are now more reluctant to use accounts that offer zero or low rates of interest. Two recent trends have become apparent. The first is towards the offer by all institutions of interest-bearing deposit accounts that are very similar, and the second is the attempt to differentiate the accounts of each institution by offering a number of ancillary services. The same has happened on the asset side of bank balance sheets. To put the same point in a different way, one could talk of an increasing service content and a trend towards packaging.

The high nominal interest rates experienced in the United Kingdom over the last decade, has led the sophisticated retail customer to seek out higher interest accounts offered by banks as well as other organisations. High interest chequing accounts are now available in various forms in the United Kingdom. Most of these accounts do not stipulate a minimum limit for the size of cheques drawn. Included in the package is usually some form of plastic card. Standing and transaction charges vary across institutions. Higher rates of interest are offered by most institutions for term deposits. The competition for deposit business will intensify over the next decade, and banks will have to offer better rates on their deposits if they hope to retain market share.

Bankers throughout Europe see consumer deposits remaining a major source of funds in the future. Table 6.3 illustrates this point quite clearly. Even given the costs of providing an efficient payments and delivery system, consumer deposits will still rank as being a cheaper source of funds than 'bought-in' funds from the money markets.

Table 6.3 *Sources of Consumer Funds*

Propositions	*Percentage of respondents*	
	Disagree	*Agree*
Even considering collection costs, consumer deposits will continue to be a cheaper source of funds than money market funds	16	84
Eventually market forces will cause the aggregate cost (interest and operations) of collecting consumer deposits to equal the cost of purchasing money market funds	64	36
Smaller banks may still be able to attract low cost consumer deposits during the next ten years	47	53
Larger banks may still be able to attract low cost consumers deposits during the next ten years	37	63
The high costs of collecting consumer funds are acceptable because of cross-selling opportunities for other services	22	78

Source: Arthur Andersen & Co., *The Decade of Change* (1986, p. 33)

Banks are expected to have to compete in a more aggressive fashion if they are to maintain the bulk of this market. Emphasis on packaging, quality and relationship banking in general will be critical factors. Corporate strategy will have to address these challenges.

It is clear that more organisations will seek to compete actively in the market for consumer deposits. Those organisations offering deposit account services will include:

1. saving and/or mortgage institutions,
2. insurance and fund management companies,
3. commercial retailing companies,

4. stockbrokers and financial intermediaries,
5. commodity houses,
6. leasing/hire purchase companies,
7. postal institutions,
8. government institutions.

It is expected that by 1995 various competitors will have a significant impact in the market for consumer funds. Major inroads will be made especially by the mortgage institutions and insurance companies. As in the United Kingdom, building societies have long been perceived as the arch rivals to banks for consumer banking services. Not surprisingly, UK banks are expected to lose more market share to this group by 1995.

In the market for corporate deposits, banks will probably continue to dominate the picture. The corporate customer has four main priorities: interest rate offered, security, service charges and availability of other banking and financial services. Given the competitive threat posed by other institutions like savings and/or mortgage institutions and insurance companies, banks must ensure quality service. Interest rates offered and service charges will undoubtedly become the two most important factors. As competition increases, corporate clients will become less loyal.

Lending facilities

Between 1970 and 1987, banks throughout the world lost ground to financial institutions and other sources as a supplier of credit. In the United Kingdom, for example, banks supplied 48 per cent of total credit in 1970, whereas the figure had fallen to around 40 per cent by 1987. (The United States, Japanese and West German figures show a similar trend.) Other non-bank financial institutions, on the other hand, have maintained their market share in France, Germany and Japan, whereas in the United Kingdom their share increased from 29 to over 45 per cent. The overall trend implies that banks will have to compete more effectively with other groups that supply credit if they are to consolidate and improve their market position.

As in the market for funds, the consumer credit market is highly segmented. Products have been tailored to attract customers from a wide consumer base. The availability, convenience and flexibility of services offered are important factors in influencing consumer demand. Most important of all is the interest rate charged on credit facilities. Three main types of credit extended to consumers can be identified: overdraft facilities, instalment lending and home mortgages.

Overdraft facilities are most widely used in the United Kingdom – only being offered by commercial banks. The importance of this type of credit in the United Kingdom is expected to decline over the next decade, and it is estimated that both the consumer instalment credit and mortgage markets will grow somewhere in the region of between 3 and 9 per cent in real terms over the next ten years.

Credit card companies pose a major threat in UK instalment lending markets. The two market leaders, Visa and MasterCard/ Access, have over 250 million cardholders worldwide. Average debt per cardholder outstanding was approximately £1000 in 1987. If used carefully, this facility can offer the consumer revolving credit at no cost at all. The credit card companies naturally assume that customers are not too careful. Visa believes that approximately half of its outstanding balances are paid off before charges are incurred. Storecards, such as the Marks and Spencer card, with similar facilities are also widely being offered by retail organisations. Credit at the point of sale is becoming a way of life in large retail organisations. Smaller retail organisations find it easier to link up with hire purchase/finance companies that can offer a similar service.

Building societies will, if the law permits, be able to offer more in the way of instalment lending. In the United Kingdom, building societies have been restricted (up until recently) in their ability to offer this type of facility. The 1986 Building Societies Act now permits building societies to offer a limited tranche of unsecured loans. It also appears that insurance companies and stockbrokers may begin to offer instalment credit facilities but it is expected that they will obtain only a small share of the market.

In the market for home mortgages, building societies still continue to compete with bankers for the major share of the market. Despite many of these developments, banks are expected to maintain the dominant share in the market for consumer credit over the next ten years. They will no longer 'grant' loans but actively sell them. The trend will be for commercial banks to offer integrated accounts for all loans which could also be used for transactions and savings purposes. Product packaging will be critically important. Similar forces are also at work in the market for commercial credit. With securitisation (the process whereby large companies raise funds by issuing capital market instruments instead of borrowing from intermediaries) and the growing disintermediation away from the banks, large companies now have direct access to the money markets. Because of these developments, corporate banking business will start to focus on the small to medium-sized corporate clients in the United Kingdom. Building societies and leasing/hire purchase companies are also expected to make inroads into this market, although at present building societies are only empowered to lend to corporations on the security of land, and only up to certain limits. However, banks currently still retain the lions share.

Although banks still retain a dominant share of the market for credit, building societies, insurance companies and other institutions will aim to secure a larger portion. UK building societies were allowed to offer consumer loans from January 1987 onwards. This means that banks will have to market actively their services. With the help of new technology, skilled management and pertinent strategic objectives, the commercial banks will have to provide quality service packages which suit the specific credit and deposit requirements of individual customers. Banks will need to adopt active marketing strategies that are aimed at selling to target segments. If this objective cannot be met, banks will certainly lose ground to the other organisations vying for a share of their business. Table 6.4 illustrates future projections relating to commercial lending shares by 1995 and supports the above view.

Table 6.4 *Commercial Lending Share in Europe by 1995*

Type of institution	Market share (%)
Banks	50+
Savings and/or mortgage institutions	10–24
Leasing/hire purchase companies	10–24
Insurance companies	1–9
Stockbrokers and financial intermediaries	1–9
Government and its institutions	1–9

Source: Arthur Andersen & Co (1986, p. 39)

BRANCHING AND DELIVERY SYSTEMS

Technological developments over the last decade have already had a substantial impact on the core business of commercial banks. New technology is cutting costs in what has traditionally been a high cost business. The networking of computer systems has transformed the speed, accuracy and economics of payments and delivery systems. It is argued that around 75 per cent of basic transactions are capable of automation and are being automated. Now individuals can make loan applications, enquire about their balances and order a plethora of other services through automated teller machine (ATM) networks, electronic funds transfer at the point of sale (EFTPOS), or by home and/or office (HOBS) facilities. Technology is also providing management with better information. Banks in the United Kingdom are actively establishing customer information files (CIFs) and household information files (HIFs) for segmentation and marketing purposes. The demand for information is by no means one-sided. Consumers also want complete and up-to-date information. Banks need to provide information and guidance with regard to their products and services, but, they must also meet customer needs for accurate, timely on-line information. It has been suggested that because of these factors, money can be regarded as information in motion!

New technology has helped to free the customer from having to go into the bank. The growth in automated teller machines (ATMs) as shown in Table 6.5 illustrates that the number of ATMs in Europe has risen from zero in 1967 to approximately 45 000 in 1987. The most sophisticated of these machines enables the consumer to withdraw cash from a range of accounts, make deposits, enquire about balances, make transfers and pay bills, order cheque books and issue statement printouts. These services are being continually extended.

Table 6.5 *Growth in the Number of ATMs Installed in Europe*

	1982	1983	1987
Number of ATMs installed in Europe	12 500	19 000	45 000
Annual percentage growth rates	—	52%	30%

Source: Battelle International ATM Survey, 1987

As banks find they can offer a broad range of products and access new locations through this automated facility, the need for a comprehensive branch network of the traditional kind becomes less necessary. Most commentators have no doubt that the number of ATMs will continue to grow over the next decade. Banks will still own the dominant share, although building societies will offer more machines.

Electronic funds transfer at the point of sale (EFTPOS) and Home and Office Banking (HOB) systems, as already mentioned in this chapter, are less operationalised than ATM networks. Developments in EFTPOS have led to talk of the coming of the 'cashless society'. France, with over 65 thousand terminals, leads the market. In fact, French banks are committed, with the government, to one national system for electronic funds transfer based on the chip card by 1990. Approximately two-thirds of French EFTPOS terminals are bank-owned while the remainder are owned by retailers themselves, an EFTPOS initiative was set up by the main UK clearing banks in 1987 but the joint initiative appears to have petered out. Individual banks are now concentrating on developing their own experimental systems.

Experiments with HOB systems are more advanced in some countries than in others, but, with the exception of certain cash management services, a sophisticated HOBS offering a broad range of services on a national scale has not yet been developed. In the future, greater advances will be made on the home and office banking fronts. The present service is essentially first generation offering a limited range of services. If these services can be made more comprehensive, it seems likely that this type of banking could take off in a big way. The time scale is much more uncertain for HOBS than for EFTPOS. In an Arthur Andersen (1986) study respondents believed that the home banking market will not be fully developed even by 1995. As a result, attention will be focused closely on the French market.

The traditional role of the branch network is changing rapidly. In a climate of rising operating expenses and money transmission costs plus declining margins, banks are beginning to reassess the size and functions of their branches. Automated accounting and processing systems have revolutionised the back end of branch banking business. ATMs, EFT facilities and HOBS are beginning to alter the front-end.

OTHER SERVICES

Banks continually have to broaden their range of services, maintain quality and price competitively if they are to preserve their position in the market for financial services. Banks in the United Kingdom have diversified into product areas like insurance broking, stockbroking, travel agencies, estate agencies and the offering of mutual fund facilities. The major objective is for an integrated approach which enables the banker to cross-sell products and services once the customer is 'locked-in'.

In the United Kingdom, for example, bankers entered the home mortgage market in earnest in the early 1980s. Recently, they have been purchasing estate agencies which dovetail nicely with their established insurance subsidiaries. Both building societies and insurance companies have also been acquiring estate agencies. These institutions main aim is to make inroads into the new homeowner market. Buying a home is probably the most important financial transaction of most people's lives. It is also a time when individuals undertake a lot of financial commitments at the same time, like mortgage, insurance/assurance, credit, etc. This market offers substantial cross- selling opportunities, and trends in these areas are also developing in other European countries.

In recent years UK banks have also concentrated on providing a broader range of ancillary services such as:

1. off-balance sheet activities,
2. trade finance,
3. electronic banking products – EFTPOS and HOBs for both the corporate and retail banking markets,
4. securities trading and distribution,
5. advisory work,
6. insurance broking

All these services have two factors in common. First, they all generate fee income as opposed to interest income. Secondly, they each offer substantial opportunities for cross-selling services.

Banks in the United Kingdom also continue to act as financial and business advisers across a wide range of activities. On the retail side, they offer advisory services in the areas of investment and unit trusts, life and pensions business and trust work. However, the range of services is much greater on the corporate side. Corporate advice includes venture capital advice, merger and acquisition work, capital structuring and business consultancy.

References and further reading

Arthur Andersen & Co. (1986) *The Decade of Change. Banking in Europe – the Next Ten Years* (London: Lafferty).

Lewis, M.K. and Davis, K.T. (1987) *Domestic and International Banking* (Oxford: Philip Allan).

Vittas, Dimitri, Frazer, Patrick and Metaxas-Vittas, Thymi (1988) *Retail Banking Revolution*, 2nd edn (London: Lafferty).

CHAPTER 7

CHARACTERISTICS OF UK DEPOSIT BANKS

INTRODUCTION

The following chapter examines the balance sheet characteristics of the UK deposit banks as well as briefly analysing their cost, income and profitability features. The final section examines various market share measures taken for the major retail banks.

THE DEPOSIT OR RETAIL BANKS' BALANCE SHEET STRUCTURE

Table 7.1 shows the sectoral balance sheet for all UK deposit banks on 31 March 1987 as published by the Bank of England. As has already been mentioned elsewhere, these banks are those which either have extensive branch networks or participate directly in the UK clearing system. They include:

1. London clearing banks (Barclays, Coutts, Lloyds, Midland and National Westminster),
2. Scottish clearing banks (Bank of Scotland, Clydesdale and Royal Bank of Scotland,
3. Northern Ireland banks (Allied Irish, Bank of Ireland, Northern Bank and Ulster Bank),
4. Trustee Savings Bank Group,
5. Co-operative Bank plc,
6. Yorkshire Bank plc,
7. Girobank plc

These banks are collectively known as the UK clearing banks. Note that in the official statistics the Bank of England Banking

Department is classified as a retail bank, but its activities are quite different from those of the other retail banks.

Table 7.1 *Retail Banks' Balance Sheet, 31 December 1987* (£ million)

Liabilities			
Sterling deposits	157718	Sterling assets	2963
Other currency		Notes and coins	
deposits	42812	Balance with the	
Notes issued	1266	Bank of England	625
Other liabilities	39875	Market loans	31410
Bills:			
		Treasury bills and	
		others	928
		Eligible bills	5354
		Advances	117686
		Investments (UK	
		government stocks	
		and others)	9852
		Other currency assets	47776
		Miscellaneous assets	25077
Total	241671	Total	241671

Source: *Bank of England Quarterly Bulletin*, May 1988, Table 3.2

Sterling deposits dominate the liabilities side of the balance sheet whereas advances (retail and corporate overdrafts and loans) are the largest category on the assets side. Notes and coins only constitute a small proportion of total assets. The banks maintain this amount of cash which can be replenished by drawing against their accounts held at the Bank of England. Market loans are essentially short-term, large denomination loans to, or deposits with, other banks and discount houses, and money lent through brokers to the parallel markets, e.g. the local authority and finance house markets. Investments are bonds, not equities, predominantly held in the form of UK government stocks (gilts). Bills are shorter term financial assets and are mainly eligible bank bills. Other currency assets are those assets that are not denominated in sterling, like dollar denominated corporate advances, etc. Miscellaneous assets refers mainly to the property assets of the banks.

On the liabilities side of the balance sheet, as well as sterling and other currency deposits, there is the category defined as 'other liabilities'. This refers to '*capital* subscribed by (and therefore owed to) the shareholders, and accumulated profits set aside as general resources against ill-fortune or for expansion of the business (e.g. building new branches) or as special provisions against future liabilities (e.g. to pay taxes)' (Struthers and Speight, 1986 p. 45). Over 50 per cent of the 'other liabilities' comprise ordinary paid-up share capital and disclosed reserves. The remainder is made up of undisclosed reserves, general provisions, debt/equity instruments and subordinated term debt.

Clearing banks' balance sheet structures

Total assets is the most common measure used to illustrate the size of banking institutions. Barclays is currently the largest bank in the United Kingdom with assets amounting to nearly £88 billion. In fact Barclays' asset size has grown by some 10 per cent per annum since 1982. NatWest is the second largest deposit bank with assets amounting to £87 billion and has experienced a similar growth rate to its main rival. Changes in total asset size of the main UK banks are shown in Table 7.2.

Table 7.2   *Total Assets of Main UK banks* (£ billion)

	1982	1983	1984	1985	1986	1987	Compound growth per annum
Bank of Scotland	5.4	6.2	78.3	8.3	9.3	11.0	+ 15
Barclays	53.9	58.0	66.9	65.1	79.0	87.8	+ 10
Lloyds	34.4	38.4	44.0	43.8	47.8	44.9	+ 6
Midland	48.0	52.6	61.5	58.1	53.2	48.5	+ 8
NatWest	54.4	59.9	71.5	72.6	83.3	87.0	+ 10
Royal Bank of Scotland	11.1	13.4	15.0	16.6	19.1	21.7	+ 5
TSB	9.1	10.1	11.5	13.2	13.2	17.0	+ 14

Source: Morgan Stanley (1989)

What is noticeable from Table 7.2 is that Midland Bank has suffered some ups and downs during the 1980s, its 1987 asset size being only marginally larger than its 1982 position. The major reason for the fall in asset size of the Midland can be attributed to its divestment of Crocker National, its troubled US subsidiary, in 1986. All these banks have sought to promote asset growth during the 1980s through better management of their balance sheets which has entailed reducing the proportion of low margin (low profitability) assets and by actively managing the changing structure of the deposits. The banks listed in Table 7.2 have sought to place less emphasis on low margin inter-bank deposits and have all attempted to consolidate their retail deposit bases.

In addition it is important to realise that each of these banks have very significant international portfolios (overseas investment, non-sterling denominated assets) which can be affected by exchange rate levels as well as volatility. For example, when sterling is weak international assets will make a greater contribution to sterling denominated total asset growth and vice versa. Table 7.3 shows the proportion of international assets in the main deposit banks balance sheets.

Table 7.3 *International Assets as a Percentage of Total Assets*

	1982	1983	1984	1985	1986	1987
Barclays	46	47	50	44	43	47
Lloyds	49	50	54	46	47	38
Midland	67	67	70	65	61	52
NatWest	41	44	42	46	48	47
£/$ Exchange rate	1.61	1.45	1.16	1.44	1.48	1.78

Source: Morgan Stanley (1989)

The above section has dealt primarily with aggregate balance sheet positions. Now we wish to consider briefly the balance sheet make-up of individual banks. Table 7.4 provides a detailed description of the main banks' balance sheet structures. One can see that by far the largest component in the assets side is for advances. Advances comprise somewhere in the region of 70 to 80 per cent of banks' balance sheets (the only exception being for the

Table 7.4 Balance Sheet Breakdown of Individual UK Banks, 1987 (£ billion)

	Bank of Scotland 29.2.88	Barclays 31.12.87	Lloyds 31.12.87	Midland 31.12.87	NatWest 31.12.87	Royal Bank of Scotland 30.9.88	Standard Chartered 31.12.87	TSB Group 31.10.88
Assets								
Short-term assets	2.1	16.2	6.2	8.2	18.0	6.4	5.2	2.7
Interbank assets	0.2	na	na	na	na	0.4	na	na
Advances	8.2	64.1	35.7	34.4	62.9	13.8	21.8	16.5
Investments	0.2	2.7	1.6	2.4	3.6	0.5	2.1	2.4
Fixed assets	0.3	1.7	1.4	0.9	2.2	0.6	0.6	0.6
Other assets	–	3.1	–	2.6	0.3	–	–	0.3
Total	11.0	87.8	44.9	48.5	87.0	21.7	29.7	22.5
Liabilities								
Share capital	0.1	0.7	0.8	0.5	0.8	0.1	0.2	0.4
Reserves	0.4	3.4	1.6	2.0	4.1	1.2	0.6	1.4
Minorities	–	0.1	–	0.1	0.1	–	0.1	–
Subordinated loans	0.4	2.6	1.4	1.3	2.1	0.8	1.4	0.5
Debt securities	–	–	–	–	–	–	–	–
Customer deposits	7.7	73.9	40.6	41.7	76.4	11.5	27.3	19.0
Interbank deposits	1.9	na	na	na	na	7.0	na	na
Other liabilities	0.5	7.1	0.5	2.9	3.5	1.1	0.1	1.2
Total	11.0	87.8	44.9	48.5	87.0	21.7	29.7	22.5
Other information								
Market capitalisation (£m)	698	4808	2819	2382	4225	1096	1217	1695
Book value[1] (pence)	98	516	395	520	690	441	530	126
Price/book value[1] (%)	9.5	84	115.6	91.8	81	84	102	90
Return on equity[1] (%)	13.5	16.6	22.4	16.0	18	16.6	21.3	13.2
Equity/assets[1] (%)	5.6	5.6	5.4	5.3	5.3	5.9	5.0	8.4

Note: [1] Estimated on year-end totals
Source: Tables calculated from Morgan Stanley, UK Banks 1989 Review

Royal Bank of Scotland where it amounts to 63 per cent of total assets). The second most important component being that of short-term assets, usually accounting for somewhere in the region of 17 to 20 per cent of total assets with the exception of the Royal Bank of Scotland (nearly 30 per cent) and the TSB (around 12 per cent). On the liabilities side, customers deposits make up the lion's share of the total. UK banks generally do not provide a breakdown between customer and interbank (money market large denominated) deposits, although interbank deposits generally constitute around 30 per cent of total deposits. The other information at the bottom of the table shows that the market capitalisation of Barclays, NatWest, Lloyds and Midland is considerably higher than for the other main banks.

Branching and staffing

The UK banking system is undergoing considerable change in the light of increased competition from new and established competitors. The increasing competitive threat posed by the building society movement as well as other non-bank financial intermediaries and retailers has forced the UK banks to bring themselves up to date by revamping its branch network. In recent years the main clearing banks have disposed of old and ill-sited branches and have converted others into modern 'user-friendly' branches in prominent positions. Branch architecture is rapidly approaching what is considered to be the 'norm' in the United States. Bank management now sees their branch networks as efficient sales outlets where cross-selling opportunities abound. There is also considerable expenditure on new technology aimed at reducing costs and producing customer, as well as management, information systems. These systems enable banks to profile (segment) customers in order to maximise the sales of a wide variety of financial services products.

Table 7.5 shows the UK banks' staff and branch numbers up to 1987. It can be seen that all the main banks have increased their number of staff since 1982, apart from Midland. On the other hand, all banks have witnessed a decline in their number of branches.

The major reorganisations and investment in new technology has significant implications for staff numbers and costs. In particular, the pressure on wage costs and the shortage of skilled staff will continue to present the banks with substantial problems. Some argue that the control of costs, and wage costs in particular, will be one of the most serious challenges facing the UK banking industry in the 1990s.

Table 7.5 *Staffing Levels and Branch Numbers of the UK Clearing Banks*

	1982	1983	1984	1985	1986	1987	Change
UK banks average							
staff numbers							
Bank of Scotland[1]	9538	9608	9952	10771	12074	13426	+41%
Barclays	75808	74988	76500	77400	80300	82700	+8%
Lloyds	52117	53092	54163	55011	56043	59778	+15%
Midland	69042	67937	67065	66423	67732	65482	- 6%
NatWest	76826	80665	82499	81715	83321	88387	+15%
Royal Bank[2]	16240	16000	17289	18105	19008	22584	+39%
TSB[3]	24452	24690	24865	26665	29936	32050	+31%
UK banks average							
branch numbers							
Bank of Scotland[1]	567	559	554	551	550	545	- 4%
Barclays	2959	2912	2900	2874	2842	2767	- 6%
Lloyds	2284	2276	2265	2229	2152	2162	- 5%
Midland	2441	2345	2288	2311	2211	2127	- 13%
NatWest	3265	3239	3216	3190	3151	3119	- 4%
Royal Bank[2]	894	882	878	864	856	857	- 4%
TSB[3]	1610	1612	1614	1600	1576	1574	- 2%

Notes: [1] Year to end February in subsequent year
         [2] Year to end September
         [3] Year to 31 October 1987 and 20 November in previous years
Source: Morgan Stanley (1989)

COSTS, INCOME AND PROFITABILITY CHARACTERISTICS

Escalating salary costs during the early 1980s encouraged the UK banks to focus greater attention on reducing costs during the rest of the 1980s. Although staff numbers have markedly increased over this period the volume of business transacted has increased at a greater rate, thus there has been 'a genuine increase in productivity' (Morgan Stanley, 1989). This increase in productivity has been partially achieved by historically low levels of staff turnover coupled with a higher investment in technology. Some quarters, in fact, have argued that because the UK banks find it so difficult (politically unacceptable) to make widespread redundancies they have to 'throw money at technology' in order to improve labour productivity. Since the early 1980s all the main banks, apart from the TSB Group have been able to reduce their costs to income ratios. In 1987 the ratios ranged from 56.3 per cent for the Bank of Scotland to 73.1 per cent for Midland. The Scottish banks tend to have lower ratios because of their lower operating costs away from the major cities, especially London. This is especially the case for Bank of Scotland which processes the bulk of its English business in Edinburgh, and has the lowest cost/income ratios of all the major UK banks (Morgan Stanley, 1989). Increased pressure on operating costs have encouraged some banks to relocate their paper shuffling operations outside London, e.g. Barclays are currently relocating part of the processing and administrative operations to Coventry. Up to 1990 it is expected that the banks' cost to income ratios may deteriorate as a result of branch remodernisation programmes and investments in technology.

Competitive pressures in both the domestic and international banking arena have resulted in depressing net interest margins (gross interest income minus gross interest expense) and have also increased non-interest income (fees, commissions and such like) as a proportion of total income. Interest spreads, the difference between interest paid and interest earned, average around 5.5 per cent on domestic business and around 1.8 per cent on the international market.

Between 1983 and 1987 all the banks have demonstrated a decline in interest spreads which is mainly explained by the change in deposit structure over this period. Funding costs have risen because of increased reliance on the more expensive wholesale markets and yields have fallen on other assets. Banks have sought to compensate for this by shifting away from low margin corporate to higher margin personal sector business, such as mortgage lending.

As a result of increased pressures on margin business banks have responded by increasing non-interest income as a proportion of total income. They have done this by a number of ways:

1. Charging for services, that were previously provided free, e.g. arrangement fees are now common practice in the personal sector, especially relating to mortgage finance.
2. Selling ancilliary services such as insurance and various investment products.
3. Growth of fee and commission earning activities, linked to such things as estate agency business, securities transactions, etc.

Table 7.6   *Non-interest Income as a Percentage of Total Income*

	1982	1983	1984	1985	1986	1987
Bank of Scotland	20.1	20.3	23.3	24.9	25.9	26.5
Barclays	28.5	29.4	31.2	32.1	33.7	36.3
Lloyds	26.2	29.5	29.2	30.4	32.6	34.6
Midland	36.1	38.9	40.1	37.0	39.6	41.1
NatWest	24.9	29.0	30.5	29.5	39.8	38.7
Royal Bank of Scotland	26.1	27.9	29.6	33.9	34.2	35.5
TSB	20.9	16.7	17.3	18.7	22.3	26.5

Source: Morgan Stanley (1989)

Table 7.6 shows the trend of non-interest income to total income for the main UK banks during the 1980s.

For all the banks the growth in the proportion of fee income to total income has been pleasing, growing strongly not just on a relative basis to interest income, which has inevitably declined due to competitive pressures, but more significantly, on an absolute basis. (Morgan Stanley, 1989)

Despite the aforementioned pressures relating to interest income and declining spreads the substantial increase in volume of banking business during the 1980s has helped maintain bank profitability. Pre-tax profitability for the major UK banks has grown by at least 20 per cent annually, as has net attributable profits (pre-tax profit

Table 7.7 *Profits of the UK Deposit Banks* (£ million)

	1982	1983	1984	1985	1986	1987	Compound growth rate %	Pre-tax compound growth rate[1] %
Pre-tax profits before exceptional provision								
Bank of Scotland	50	59	80	95	119	157	+26	
Barclays	440	485	605	840	895	1052	+20	
Lloyds	329	419	468	561	700	818	+20	
Midland	251	225	135	351	434	511	+29	
NatWest	449	518	671	804	1011	1266	+23	
Royal Bank of Scotland	96	131	166	185	274	309	+27	
TSB	130	150	154	169	206	327	+22	
Net attributable profits								
Bank of Scotland	40	50	40	49	72	82	+18	+26
Barclays	310	272	285	440	633	185	+10	+20
Lloyds	248	276	230	410	497	227	na	+20
Midland	145	114	45	122	242	393	na	+29
NatWest	398	396	289	442	614	442	+17	+23
Royal Bank of Scotland	81	73	95	119	129	193	+21	+27
TSB	55	35	81	97	132	178	+38	+22

Source: Morgan Stanley (1989)
Note: [1] Before exceptional LDC provisions

minus tax, minorities and extraordinary items *but* excluding exceptional items). Table 7.7 illustrates the profit being generated by both domestic and international banking business.

It can be seen that the pre-tax profit performance, in terms of growth, during the 1980s has been quite similar for the banks, NatWest being the most profitable followed by Barclays. The pre-tax profitability of the domestic operations of NatWest increased by 31 per cent annually between 1982 and 1987 compared with 25 per cent for Barclays, 26 per cent for Midland and 29 per cent for Lloyds. NatWest is now viewed as the top bank in terms of both domestic and total pre-tax profits. Profits gleaned from international business are much more variable than from domestic business, thus reflecting the unpredictable performance of overseas subsidiaries which are subject to exceptional provisioning on LDC exposures as well as the impact of exchange rate changes. During the 1980s NatWest has performed relatively well, although Barclays has had problems in the United States, Middle East, Hong Kong and Europe; Lloyds has had difficulties in the Far East and Midlands' results were severely affected by the atrocious performance of its US Crocker Bank in 1983 and 1984.

A NOTE ON MARKET SHARES

By the end of 1987 the Committee of London and Scottish Bankers (CLSB) held 37.9 per cent of the UK private sector deposits, compared with 41.6 per cent for the building societies. These figures suggest that the banks and building societies have an approximately equal share of the sterling deposit market but this is misleading because the CLSB Groups' deposits includes a substantial proportion of interbank and corporate deposits whereas the building society deposits are predominantly retail.

If one considers personal deposits, building societies dominate the market holding well over 50 per cent compared with the CLSB banks' 23 per cent in 1987. On the other hand banks provide two thirds of consumer credit whereas building societies have only recently been permitted to enter this market. Building societies, as we well know, still dominate the housing finance market. Corporate deposit taking and advances are still predominantly the preserve of the main clearers. Table 7.8 provides an illustration of the sterling deposits and advances breakdowns for the CLSB banks.

Table 7.8 *Market Shares: Sterling Deposits and Sterling Advances* (per cent)

	Sterling deposits				Sterling advances			
	1985	1986	1987	1988	1985	1986	1987	1988
Bank of Scotland	4.1	4.0	4.1	4.5	4.8	4.9	4.8	5.0
Barclays	23.7	22.3	23.7	24.8	25.6	23.0	24.1	25.7
Lloyds	17.8	15.7	15.5	14.6	17.1	16.0	15.8	15.0
Midland	16.5	16.2	14.5	14.4	17.0	17.0	15.3	14.5
NatWest	29.7	27.3	25.8	25.1	26.3	24.7	25.0	24.4
Royal Bank of Scotland	6.1	5.6	6.2	5.6	7.1	6.8	6.7	6.2
Standard Chartered	2.1	2.2	2.1	1.8	2.2	2.5	2.7	2.2
TSB	—	6.8	8.1	9.1	—	5.1	5.5	6.9
Total	100.0	100.0	100.0	100.0	100.0	100.0	100.0	100.0

Source: Estimated from Committee of London Scottish Bankers (1989)

CURRENT ISSUES FACING UK BANKS

UK banks did well in 1988 and reported substantial increases in their pre-tax profits for the year. But despite the healthy performance, the banks are being brought to account for the way they conduct their business. The four main clearing banks have been forced to introduce interest bearing current accounts in order to compete with the building societies. These new accounts are likely to have a substantial impact on the profits of the clearers. It is estimated that in the case of NatWest, the probable fall in profits resulting from the introduction of these accounts amounts to around £70 million, 5 per cent of the bank's 1988 pre-tax profits of £1.4 billion. For Midland, these new accounts will cost around £15 million, more than 2 per cent of 1988's £693 million pre-tax profits.

More business costs loom for the banks. The independent report into banking services by Professor Robert Jack calls for wide reaching and potentially costly changes for UK banks. The two year inquiry, published in February 1989, contained 83 recommendations aimed at clarifying the law covering a wide range of banking activities, ranging from cheque clearance to electronic cash dispensers. Among proposals to safeguard customer confidentiality the report highlighted the need for a clear statutory definition of the banks' duty to observe customer confidentiality and details of the circumstances in which it can be breached. Another important recommendation called for the banks to itemise their charges, including those for standard bank accounts. Three new statutes were demanded, including a Banking Services Act. The report also suggested that the liability for 'phantom' withdrawals from cash dispensers should be split between the customer and the bank – unless negligence could be proved by either party, a £50 liability limit for customers on unauthorised cashpoint withdrawals was suggested. Finally, a Cheques and Bank Payment Orders Act should be introduced to take account of a new proposal for a non-negotiable, non-transferable cheque, called a Bank Payment Order, designed to reduce the possibility of fraud.

Many of the proposals of the 'Jack Report' – in particular the elements to safeguard customer confidentiality and the proposed introduction of the new payment order – will involve heavy expenditure for the banks.

While the Jack Report could have long term and far reaching effects on the banking industry, in the short term the key considerations for the UK clearers in 1989 and beyond will be taken up by:

1. competition,
2. costs,
3. capital,
4. Europe and 1992.

Competition will continue to intensify among the banks, while the building societies continue to compete aggressively for the banks' retail business. The most successful banks will be the banks that can attract market share, turn the new business into profit and generate above average returns on equity. As was mentioned earlier in this chapter, the UK clearers have consistently found it difficult to contain costs. The Scottish banks and Lloyds have the lowest cost to income ratios which are probably sustainable. NatWest and Barclays, the two largest clearers, have the ability to improve their cost to income ratios, but they may find this difficult in the light of a slow-down in business growth.

In terms of meeting the new 'Basle' capital requirements (see Chapter 8), the UK banks are well-off, probably over-capitalised by EC standards. Estimated Bank for International Settlements (BIS) ratios show all the main UK banks to be in relatively strong positions. Nevertheless, a policy of expansion abroad could force the banks to look to their shareholders. In the case of the TSB more capital could be required if it continues to grow at its present rate. If LDC loans require additional provisioning the capital ratios of Lloyds and Midland will be the worst affected.

One of the most important strategic issues taxing the minds of many banks at the moment is how to adopt a successful strategy for 1992 and beyond (see Chapters 11 and 12). Barclays and Midland have the most significant European presence at the moment and seem set to gain most from the single market in financial services. Some sources suggest that NatWest and Lloyds don't regard Europe as a high priority, something that senior management would dispute. The remaining clearers, with the exception of the Royal Bank of Scotland which has engineered a (defensive?) cross-equity shareholding in Banco Santander, have no strong European ambitions.

References and further reading

Committee of London and Scottish Bankers (1989) *Abstract of Banking Statistics,* vol. 6, May.

Molyneux, P. (1989) 'Altered states', *International Correspondent Banker,* March/April, pp. 32–3.

Morgan Stanley (1989) *United Kingdom Banks 1989 Review,* January.

Morgan Stanley (1988) 'Financial services companies one year after the crash', *Financial Services Commentary,* 3rd edn, November.

Struthers, J. and Speight, M. (1986) *Money, Institutions, Theory and Policy,* (Longman: London).

CHAPTER 8

THE CENTRAL BANK AND BANK REGULATION

INTRODUCTION

The purpose of this chapter is to outline the main functions of a central bank, examine the operations of the Bank of England and discuss banking regulation in the United Kingdom. The first part of this chapter deals with the main functions of a central bank and also considers the history and organisational set-up of the Bank of England. Many authors have provided excellent descriptions of these functions and organisational features and subsequently the format of the first part of this chapter borrows heavily from Goacher (1986) and to a lesser extent Struthers and Speight (1986). The second part of this chapter looks at why banks are regulated, the scope and tools of bank supervision and recent developments in UK and international bank supervision.

FUNCTIONS OF A CENTRAL BANK

Before we consider the main functions of a central bank it is best to provide a definition of such an institution. A central bank can generally be defined as a body that undertakes the financial operations of the government, which in so doing, influences the behaviour of financial institutions in order to aid the economic policy of the government. The main functions of a central bank can be listed as follows:

1. The central bank controls the issue of notes and coin (legal tender). Usually, the central bank will have a monopoly of the issue, although this is not essential as long as the central bank

has power to restrict the amount of private issues of notes and coins.

2. It has the power to control the amount of credit-money created by banks. In other words, it has the power to control, by either direct or indirect means, the money supply.

3. A central bank should also have control over non-bank financial intermediaries which provide credit, although it should be noted that the Bank of England has no control over building societies, neither prudentially or for monetary policy purposes.

4. Encompassing both parts (b) and (c), the central bank should effectively use the relevant tools and instruments of monetary policy so as to control:

   (a) credit expansion,
   (b) liquidity, and (subsequently),
   (c) the money supply of an economy.

5. 'It must be able to support as well as control the financial system in order to prevent crises of confidence and violent, disruptive changes in the supply and cost of credit. It must be able to relieve shortages as well as prevent excesses' (Struthers and Speight, 1986, p. 18).

6. A central bank will act as the Government's banker. It will hold the Government's bank account and will perform certain traditional banking operations for the Government, such as taking deposits and lending. In its capacity as banker to the Government it will manage and administer the country's National Debt.

7. The central bank will also act as the official agent to the Government in dealing with all its gold and foreign exchange matters. The Government reserves of gold and foreign exchange will be held at the central bank. A central bank will at times intervene in the foreign exchange markets, at the behest of the Government, in order to influence the exchange value of the domestic currency. For example, in May 1987, the German, Japanese and UK central banks intervened in the foreign exchange markets to influence the exchange value of the dollar. 'It will maintain contact with other central banks and international financial institutions and will conduct, or at least play a part in or advise on, negotiations

with them' (Struthers and Speight, 1986, p. 19). This point can be illustrated by the recent 'Convergence Agreement' between the Bank of England and the Federal Reserve in January 1987, which set uniform capital adequacy standards for American and UK banks. (This in fact has now been superseded by the Bank for International Settlements capital adequacy standards – see Chapter 11.)

THE BANK OF ENGLAND

The Bank of England is the central bank of the United Kingdom. Very generally, a central bank is ultimately responsible for the organisation of its country's official monetary and financial policies. This, of course, includes the supervision of banking institutions; monetary policy; banker to the Government and general overseer of the whole financial system.

The origin of the Bank of England can be traced back to 1694 when it received its charter as a joint stock company. The Bank, in fact, was established in order to improve the fund raising capability of the British government. It was not until the Bank Charter Act of 1844, however, that the Bank of England obtained full central bank status. The 1844 Act ultimately led to a monopoly for the Bank in the production of notes and coins in the United Kingdom.

During the nineteenth century the Bank of England consolidated its position as overseer of the British banking system by standing ready to purchase bills of exchange issued by other commercial banks, if the need arose. This lender-of-last-resort function helped maintain public confidence and credibility in the banking system. In fact, during the nineteenth century the Bank of England found itself performing many of the functions that are today thought commonplace for a central bank; the main issuer of bank notes and coins; lender-of-last-resort; banker to the government and to other domestic banks; and guardian of the nation's official reserves. It must be remembered, however, that although the Bank of England performed these functions (as well as undertaking a larger role in the financial management of the economy) it still remained a private joint stock company, operating for a profit. The Bank of England Act of 1946 nationalised the Bank and the state acquired all of the Bank's capital.

Constitution of the Bank

Like other nationalised organisations, the Bank of England is a public corporation free to manage its own activities independently. However, because of its important role with regard to the implementation of monetary policy and overall supervision of the financial system, the actual degree of operational freedom is quite limited. The Bank of England is managed by a Court of Directors, which comprises the Governor (presently Robin Leigh-Pemberton, former Chairman of National Westminster Bank), the Deputy Governor, four full-time executive directors and twelve part-time directors. All these posts are appointments made on the recommendation of the Prime Minister.

Functions and organisational structure of the Bank of England

The Report of the Wilson Committee (1980) summarised the broad responsibilities of the Bank of England:

> The Bank has a very wide range of functions, probably wider than those of the central bank of any other major industrial country. It is responsible for the execution of monetary policy, the management of the national debt and the note circulation and administration of the Exchange Equalisation Account. It is used also to be responsible for the administration of exchange controls . . . it acts as banker both to the banking sector and to the government. It provides advice on economic policy to the Chancellor and the Prime Minister. Finally, it has a specific statutory responsibility for supervision of the banking sector and a more diffuse responsibility as guardian of the good order of the financial system as a whole.

In its operations, the Bank's activities are divided into 3 main areas; banking supervision, operations and corporate services; finance and industry and policy and markets. (The following are all listed in Goacher, 1986, ch. 6.)

Banking supervision, operations and corporate services
    1. *Banking Supervision Division*: this is responsible for the prudential regulation (or supervision) of all authorised banking institutions as defined by the Banking Act 1987.

2. *Banking Department*: undertakes normal banking services to private individuals and corporate customers. This, of course, includes the banking facilities offered through the Bank of England to commercial banks.
3. *Registrars Department*: 'maintains registers of holdings of government and other stocks, and is responsible for the servicing of this debt' (Goacher, 1986, ch. 6, p. 116).
4. *Printing Works*: prints new and destroys old bank notes.
5. *Corporate Services*: responsible for the management of the Bank's property assets, provision of computer services and also produces the Bank's accounts.

Finance and industry
1. *Financial Supervision – General Division*: responsible for supervision in the fields of institutional development and techniques in banking.
2. *Industrial Finance Division*: responsible for supervision of developments in industrial finance and the co-ordination of the industrial liaison work of the Bank.

Policy and markets
1. *Economics*: macroeconomic model building and forecasting.
2. *Financial Statistics*: data collection and interpretation.
3. *Gilt-edged Market*: general operations in the gilt-edged securities market and facilitation of longer-term government borrowing.
4. *Money Markets*: daily operations in the discount market and general supervision of short-term money markets.
5. *Foreign Exchange*: responsible for operations in the foreign exchange and gold markets, the running of the Exchange Equalisation Account and the implementation of exchange rate policy.
6. *Territorial/International*: monitoring of overseas financial developments and the maintenance of contacts with other central banks and international monetary institutions.
7. *Information*: public relations and publications.

The above broadly outlines the functions and organisational structure of the Bank of England.

Banking role of the Bank of England
The Bank of England provides a broad range of mainstream banking products and services to its customers. However, the customer base of the Bank of England is considerably different from that of the typical commercial banks.

1. Private customers: mainly the Bank's staff and a few domestic institutions and private individuals.
2. Overseas central banks and international organisations: the Bank holds accounts for over 100 overseas institutions, including the Bank for International Settlements, the World Bank and the International Monetary Fund.
3. Banks and other financial institutions: the Bank holds a large amount of banker's deposits. Eighty per cent of these are compulsory non-interest bearing cash ratio deposits, held for liquidity purposes. The remainder are mainly voluntary clearing bank deposits held to facilitate interbank funds flows arising from the cheque clearing process.
4. British Central Government: the balances of the government's accounts are centralised at the Bank of England. The Bank must ensure that any net deficit is financed and that surplus funds are used to repay outstanding debt. Long-term net deficits are financed through the issuance of gilt-edged securities, whereas shorter-term funding comes via issues of Treasury bills.

National debt management
You can see from the above that the Bank acts as banker to the British Central Government and also has responsibility for managing the country's national (public sector) debt. As a result, the Bank has to arrange the funding of the public sector borrowing requirement, usually termed the PSBR. (Note that the PSBR is merely the difference between government revenues and government expenditures as planned in the annual budgets. If expenditures exceed revenues then we have a positive PSBR and if expenditures are less than revenues we have a negative PSBR.) Not only does the Bank have to arrange the annual funding of the PSBR, but it also has to fund outstanding government debt. In other words, it has to fund a continual stream of maturing instruments, whether they be gilt-edged stock or Treasury bills.

The Bank chooses a mix of debt instruments to offer for sale so as to manage the characteristics of the outstanding national debt. It does this with some particular policy objectives in mind. In addition to the relatively straightforward sale or redemption (repurchase) of government debt, the Bank of England may undertake open-market operations. This is where the Bank enters the gilt-edged or Treasury bill market and buys or sells the instruments in order to influence the financial assets portfolio held by the private sector. (We will discuss open market operations in a little more detail later on.)

Production and distribution of bank notes
This function is self-explanatory and therefore does not need to be discussed here.

Lender-of-last-resort
The Bank of England has acted as lender-of-last-resort for the banking system for over a century. This means that the Bank stands ready to supply funds to the banking sector if liquidity or (much worse) solvency problems arise. 'However, this does not mean that the Bank guarantees the solvency of every banking institution in the United Kingdom . . . Rather, the situation is that the Bank stands ready to accommodate shortages of cash in the banking sector, perhaps resulting from increased demands for cash from the non-bank private sector, or from an unusually large net flow of funds from private bank accounts to the government's accounts at the Bank of England' (Goacher, 1986, ch. 6, p. 119). This view espouses a short-term view of the lender-of-last-resort. It is argued that the Bank, in its role as lender-of-last-resort, is not prepared to guarantee the solvency of every banking institution because this would encourage bankers to take undue risks and operate imprudently, especially if banks knew that they would be bailed out (by taxpayers' money) if they became insolvent.

In general, the Bank may act as lender-of-last-resort either by lending on a secured basis direct to the banking sector, or by purchasing (rediscounting) short-term paper, namely commercial or Treasury bills, from the banking sector. Almost invariably, the assistance is provided via the discount houses, although recently, the Bank of England bailed out Johnson Matthey Bankers in 1984 by lending direct. In fact, in extreme cases, the Bank of England will offer direct support to a bank in trouble. The largest 'support' operation ever mounted by the Bank came in 1973/74 with the 'joint support operation' (often referred to as the 'lifeboat'). Here, the Bank organised help, together with the main clearing banks, for 26 fringe (or secondary) banks facing severe liquidity problems. A more recent example of Bank assistance is the rescue operation organised for Johnson Matthey Bankers (JMB) in September 1984. Here, the Bank purchased JMB for £1 (yes, one pound) and pledged £150 million worth of indemnities, which JMB could call upon.

Foreign exchange transactions
As we mentioned earlier, the Bank manages the Treasury's Exchange Equalisation Account. This Account contains the UK's gold, sterling and foreign currency reserves. These can be used for the Bank's foreign currency exchange market intervention if it wishes to alter exchange rates for macroeconomic policy purposes. When the sterling exchange rate was fixed (most of the period between 1945 and 1972) the Bank had to actively manage the Account so as to maintain parity. For example, if there was pressure on sterling to depreciate then the Bank would intervene and buy sterling with foreign currency reserves from the Account, thus increasing demand for sterling and helping to maintain the fixed rate. Even in a floating exchange rate system the Bank will still intervene at times to smooth out exchange rate movements.

Monetary policy
Probably the most important function of any central bank is to undertake monetary control operations. As you should realise, monetary control operations aim to control the amount of money (money supply) in the economy. These operations differ according to the monetary policy objectives they aim to achieve. This, of course, is determined by the government's overall macroeconomic policies.

In the United Kingdom, the monetarist stance of the government's macroeconomic policy between 1979 and 1985 emphasised the importance of the monetary policy role. It has been argued that the success or failure of the government's macroeconomic policy over this period depended crucially upon the efficiency with which the Bank undertook its monetary control responsibilities.

The Bank has various means by which it can influence the amount of money in the economy. These operational methods and instruments can be summarised as follows:

1. *Open market operations*: where the Bank operates in the market and buys or sells government debt to the non-bank private sector. In general, if the Bank sells government debt the money supply decreases (all other things being equal) and vice versa. As a result, the Bank can influence the portfolio of assets held by the private sector. This will influence the level of liquidity within the financial system and will also affect the level and structure of interest rates.

2. *Lender-of-last-resort*: as we have already seen, the Bank of England may also lend funds directly to the banking sector through its function as lender-of-last-resort.

3. *Implementation of non-market controls*:
   (a) *Special deposits*: these are funds that commercial banks are required to hold at the Bank of England and are equal to a certain percentage of a subcategory of their sterling deposits. Special deposits were used as a tool of monetary control throughout the 1960s and 1970s. Although the Bank paid interest on the special deposits they did not constitute reserve assets and subsequently could not be used as part of the reserve base. A call by the Bank for special deposits essentially reduced the bank's ability to create credit. The Bank has made no call for special deposits since 1983.

   (b) *Supplementary special deposits*: known as the 'CORSET'. This tool of monetary control was used throughout the 1970s. These were essentially extra deposits that commercial banks had to place in the Bank on top of the special deposits; if they exceeded specified maximum target growth rates for a category of interest-bearing sterling deposits. Supplementary special deposits paid no interest. The supplementary special deposits scheme was abolished in June 1980.

   (c) *Reserve requirements*: minimum cash or liquid asset reserve ratios had to be held by banks during most of the post-war period up until 1981. You should remember from Chapter 2 that any restriction placed on a bank's cash and/or liquidity ratio would inhibit its ability to create credit.

(d) *Formal directives*: throughout the 1960s and 1970s, the Bank issued formal directives to the banking sector. These included directives on: interest ceilings on deposits; quantitative guidelines such as lending ceilings; qualitative guidelines such as encouraging banks to lend to certain sectors of the economy.

(e) *Moral suasion*: probably the most effective control has been that of 'moral suasion' where the Bank of England has 'persuaded' (coerced) banks to follow certain directives.

BANKING REGULATION IN THE UNITED KINGDOM

Why regulate banks?

Bank regulation is usually justified in terms of one of the following three considerations; to ensure that banks are safe so as to help preserve the overall financial stability of the economy and to provide adequate 'consumer protection' to depositors; it is often justified by a policy desire to control the monetary system; and finally, banking regulation is sometimes imposed on the grounds that it is necessary to protect financial markets from being inherently uncompetitive. In this latter respect regulation should seek to restrict the build up of monopoly power and reduce concentration in financial markets. The main concern of the remainder of this chapter is with the first of these justifications, or rationales, for bank regulation.

It is a fact that banks have traditionally attracted significant public regulation, mainly because of the important role they have to play in society. Moreover, the survival of financial institutions, particularly of banks, is influenced greatly by the confidence of the public in the soundness of their operations. Thus, the social consequences of large and widespread banking failures are generally viewed as sufficient justification for some form of supervision, or prudential regulation, of banking activities.

In order to maintain confidence within the system, banks must ensure that they are always able to meet legitimate demands for funds by depositors and borrowers, and this obligation requires the banks' adherence to appropriate standards of liquidity and capital adequacy. Effective supervision should attempt to maintain these standards both formally and informally in order to enhance and preserve confidence within the banking system. This is particularly important in a system like that of the United Kingdom, which has strong international links. In the past, it has been shown that some banks have weakened their prudential standards under competitive pressure and in the search for higher profits.

One of the primary objectives of an effective system of supervision should be to minimise the social cost of intermediation consistently with protecting depositors. The supervisory system should also help to ensure that banks do not follow imprudent policies to the extent that their operational viability, or solvency, is threatened. Excessive risk taking by banks and undue risk aversion should both be discouraged. An effective supervisory system should attempt to combine flexibility and realism with safety and self-discipline. Although these objectives are easy to specify, they are difficult to obtain within a free enterprise banking system. To see how far these goals are achieved by the UK and other supervisory authorities one must review the scope of bank supervision.

Scope of bank supervision

The foremost aim of the supervisory authorities, therefore, is to help ensure confidence (thereby protecting depositors) within the banking system. In this setting, smaller and newer institutions, the lesser known names, are usually of particular interest to the authorities, although recent US experiences have shown that large bank failures (like Franklin National) can occur in modern financial systems. To enable the authorities to achieve these important safety goals, some type of monitoring and control system must be chosen and two main approaches are distinguishable in conventional bank supervisory systems. In some countries the prudential regulations are laid down in great detail as mandatory prescriptions, whereas in others regulations are informally spelled out by agreements between the supervisory authorities and the individual banks.

Not only are there two types of supervisory system, there are also two specific types of tool used by the authorities. First of all there are various licensing requirements prescribed by statute which financial institutions must observe in order to maintain their status within the financial spectrum. These requirements specify certain factors which institutions must comply with if they wish to qualify for 'bank' or any other form of financial status; that is, to obtain a banking licence. The supervisory authorities are concerned here with the kinds of business credit institutions may undertake, the competence of the institutions' management and various other factors that may affect the 'soundness' of the banking system.

The other form of control is prudential regulation, which is concerned with the maintenance of balance sheet ratios. It can be said that supervisory authorities generally have shown an historical preference for some form of ratio analysis in evaluating bank soundness. Consequently, these authorities are now predominantly concerned with the maintenance of various prudential ratios, usually capital and liquidity ratios.

Tools of supervision

Over the last two decades, supervisory authorities have increasingly turned to ratio analysis for evaluating bank soundness. The reason is probably that the implied numerical precision is reassuring in an area of great potential uncertainty. Although it has never been the general view of regulators that ratio results should be taken at face value, the fact remains that they have always found ratios more useful in practice than alternative measures.

Historically, US banks and regulators have been the forerunners in using ratios as supervisory tools, although the Comptroller of the Currency officially de-emphasised ratios in the early 1960s. Supervisors have been concerned with the measurement of one, several or all of the following:

1. *Capital adequacy*: this entails an evaluation of the capital cushion, or net worth, related to a bank's risk exposure. In general, capital adequacy appraisal may be taken to be synonymous with bank solvency assessments. A bank's capital cushion is generally regarded as a protective internal fund against unforeseen and unexpected financial pressures of significant magnitude.

2. *Asset quality*: loans constitute the major component in assessing asset quality. This is because loans are invariably a bank's main earning asset.
3. *Management and earnings*: earnings and management/administration assessments are judged in relation to other facets of the business.
4. *Liquidity*: liquidity is a key factor because a bank must be able to meet both normal and abnormal shortfalls in anticipated cash flows. Although the central bank support function may come into play in banking liquidity analysis, supervisory schemes have still attempted to gauge and test a bank's prudential liquidity positions. It is not a central bank function to bail out illiquid and imprudent banks.

However, a certain amount of trial and error was necessary before the use of ratios as satisfactory regulatory tools could be applied to any of the above problems. (In fact, by the mid-1980s many regulators were turning to more dynamic 'cash flow' approaches to monitoring supervisory requirements.)

Domestic bank supervision

UK banks have traditionally been subject to a variety of non-supervisory regulatory controls exercised by the Bank of England. These regulatory controls are primarily for monetary and credit policy purposes in the context of the overall macroeconomic management of the economy; they are not designed for supervisory purposes. Up to the early 1980s, for example, UK banks were subject to a number of lending controls, both direct and market-orientated. Modern domestic banking supervision really developed in the aftermath of the 1973/74 secondary banking crisis. The Bank of England believes that the most effective regulatory arrangements combine appropriate elements of self-discipline and law. In this context the modern Bank philosophy is a flexible, legal one.

A landmark in the modern evolution of UK domestic bank supervision was the 1979 Banking Act. It represented the first legal codification of the Bank of England's regulatory powers. One important impetus was the December 1977 adoption in Brussels of the First Directive of the EC on the co-ordination of laws, regulations and administrative provisions concerning the taking up and pursuit of the business of credit institutions (document 77/80/ EEC). Nevertheless, the rapid evolution of UK supervision during the 1970s had exposed serious weaknesses in the old system. The new Act strengthened the powers of the Bank in areas previously shown to be weak. It also formalised the powers of UK banking supervisors and removed uncertainties concerning the Bank of England's authority and scope of supervision.

UK supervision has tended to concentrate specifically on two main areas of banking:

1. the entry and establishment of banks,
2. the risk and corresponding return properties of a bank's portfolio of activities.

The 1979 Act was more specific on the supervision of these two areas, but it did not break fundamentally with earlier 1970s philosophy and corresponding supervisory practice. The legislation was similar in many respects to the relevant bank supervisory laws in other European countries, and this was a reflection in part of the need to conform with EC requirements for eventual harmonisation. Banks were required to be authorised under this new Act, and specific criteria were laid down for this purpose. Until the 1979 Banking Act the authorisation or licensing of institutions in the United Kingdom to conduct banking business was a very loosely structured process. Up to 1973, for example, the secondary banks were hardly supervised at all. In one sense, this loophole was one contributor to the 1973/74 secondary banking crisis.

The 1979 Banking Act defined those institutions subject to the Act, and it specified the criteria that must be satisfied to obtain Bank of England authorisation. The Act gave the Bank statutory authority to supervise all authorised institutions; it also controlled the use of banking names and descriptions. Under the Act the Bank of England was empowered to authorise banks as either LDTs (licensed deposit takers) or recognised banks. The Act laid down the procedure for revocation and recognition of a licence. One practical problem with the Act had been the distinction between licensed deposit takers and recognised banks. Although this distinction was based on the range of business conducted, it had been argued by some institutions that it represented a 'sheep and goats' approach. They argued that it implied that LDTs were somehow inferior institutions, although the Bank of England strenuously denied this intention of the authorisation system. The distinction has been abandoned by the 1987 Banking Act following the 1984/85 problems of JMB (Johnson Matthey Bankers). (Licensed deposit takers were more stringently supervised than recognised banks, but it was a recognised bank, JMB, that encountered much publicised difficulties following the 1979 Act.)

The Bank of England monitors the risk and return properties of banks' activities through the use of capital adequacy and liquidity ratios. The most detailed supervisory rules in this area are for capital adequacy, although the Bank emphasises the singular importance of prudential liquidity to sound banking. The Bank of England identifies the following important purposes for which capital is required:

1. to promote a cushion to absorb losses,
2. to demonstrate to potential depositors the willingness of the shareholders to put their own funds at risk on a permanent basis,
3. to provide resources free of financing costs,
4. to be a suitable form of finance for the general infrastructure of the business.

Only shareholders' funds (equity and reserves or own funds) are regarded as suitable for all these purposes. From 1975 the Bank has supplemented its gearing ratio (capital:deposits) with a more detailed risk-assets scheme. The objective of the gearing ratio is to ensure that the capital position of an institution is regarded as acceptable by its depositors and other creditors. For these purposes, the gearing ratio may be computed from published data. The risk assets approach is designed to test the adequacy of capital in relation to the risk of losses which may be sustained.

The Bank has emphasised the concept of free capital, or free resources, within the capital ratios that it monitors. Free (or adjusted) capital is essentially total capital less fixed assets and other specified deductibles. The Bank of England in recent years has emphasised more strongly the concept of primary capital in supervisory capital adequacy ratios. Primary capital refers to capital of the highest quality. Detailed rules have been laid down by the Bank regarding the inclusion of subordinated debt and other

philosophy of dialogue and participation. The approach eventually adopted by the Bank is the product of this process of dialogue. In this context the Bank sees its role as 'honest broker' in the formulation of supervisory rules. Dialogue between the Bank and supervised institutions enables the Bank to distill the opinions and experiences of all market participants. To this extent the Bank acts as a kind of proxy for a well-informed market.

The post-1979 UK system is now subject to a considerable volume of new changes partially as a result of the JMB difficulties in 1984 and 1985. A new Banking Act 1987 has been passed by Parliament, and many of its provisions are linked to the Financial Services Act 1986, which legislates for the regulation of the investment industry. The Banking Act institutes the setting up of a new Board of Banking Supervision to assist the Governor of the Bank in his supervisory responsibilities. The objective is to draw on the expertise of independent commercial banking experience at the highest level.

The other main proposals of the 1987 Act can be summarised as follows:

1. the 1979 Act two-tier system (of LDTs and recognised banks) will be replaced with a single set of criteria for bank authorisation,
2. in order to call themselves banks, institutions must have a minimum paid-up capital of at least £5 million,
3. although the Bank rejected the principle of routine inspection, it was deemed appropriate to increase its statutory powers and resources,
4. bank auditors are to be drawn more closely into the supervisory process under a guideline (rather than statutory) basis,
5. the misreporting of information to the Bank will become a criminal offence,
6. banks will be obliged by law to report large exposures, and limits (in relation to its capital) will be placed on a bank's exposure to a single borrower or connected group of borrowers,
7. deposit definitions will be amended to take account of the growing array of new instruments.

UK bank regulation – the international dimension

The special position of London and the international banking orientation of banks during the 1970s stimulated growing UK concern with international bank supervision. It is clear that many banking problems and risks have emanated from the international financial arena. Structural developments like internationalisation and globalisation (discussed in Chapter 9) have also questioned the practical reality of insulating a domestic supervisory system like that of the United Kingdom from wider international developments. Banking and finance are no longer confined by such artificial political boundaries.

As a result of various pressures the important banking nations of the world have moved closer throughout the 1980s to a common approach towards bank supervisory regulation and an internationally agreed standard. The process of international supervisory cooperation that culminated in the December 1987 report prepared by the Bank for International Settlements Basle Committee on Banking Regulations and Supervisory Practices was a long and complex one. It is also part of a continuing process that must tackle any unresolved issues and also have the adaptability to meet the new challenges that will undoubtedly emerge in the developing global financial arena. The early work of the Basle Committee on Banking Regulations and Supervisory Practices – known first at the 'Blunden Committee' and later the 'Cooke Committee' – during the 1960s and 1970s was enshrined in the 1975 Basle Concordat. This agreed code placed the primary responsibility for the supervision of international bank solvency on the supervisory authority of the parent bank's home country. By the end of the 1970s most major banking nations had expended considerable efforts in refining their own national supervisory capital adequacy systems. Many major European countries tended to favour the risk-assets approach for monitoring and regulating bank capital adequacy. Italy and Luxembourg in Europe and major non-European countries like the United States, Japan and Canada used the gearing ratio approach. These inconsistencies made international comparisons difficult; they also obscured the possibility of differential regulatory impacts in capital adequacy regulation.

In 1978 the Basle Committee recommended that the solvency of domestically headquartered banks should be appraised on a consolidated basis. The 1975 Basle Concordat was substantially revised in May 1983: a central theme in this revision was that each bank's worldwide business should be regulated and supervised on a consolidated basis. The Council of European Communities issued a 1983 directive that recommended the supervision of credit institutions on a consolidated basis, and the principle of consolidated supervision has been given legal backing in EC countries during recent years.

Capital adequacy began to dominate international supervisory concern during the 1980s. The 1982 debt crisis initiated major efforts by supervisory authorities to improve capital adequacy ratios. The need also grew for common international ground rules in order to compare different national capital adequacy systems. From 1984 the Cooke Committee set about developing the basis for a common standard for capital adequacy. But the January 1987 bilateral agreement between the Bank of England and the Board of Governors of the US Federal Reserve System became for a while the important focal point for the international convergence of capital adequacy. It was an historic initiative.

The January 1987 agreement was reached in a matter of months. This speed reflected the priority assigned to it by the respective central banks. International banks had also been increasingly critical of the apparent capital-adequacy regulation asymmetries between banks in international financial markets. The US/UK convergence agreement built on the earlier work of the Basle Committee. The proposal was for a common risk-asset system for capital adequacy. The US/UK proposals have now been shelved in the light of the December 1987 proposals by the BIS Committee on Banking Regulations and Supervisory Practices. The aim of these new proposals is to unify capital adequacy amongst banks in the industrialised world. A key feature of the BIS proposals is that by the end of 1992 all banks with any significant international business will be required to maintain a minimum capital:risk assets ratio.

The Basle proposals and EC legislation

The Basle Committee's December 1987 proposals were ratified in July 1988 and they reflect the culmination of its important work in the international convergence of capital adequacy. The Committee was charged by the Group of Ten (largest ten industrialised countries in the world) or G-10 central bank governors to seek a common approach among its members towards measuring capital adequacy and the prescription of minimum capital standards. The Basle proposals for convergence of capital adequacy are based on a risk-assets ratio (RAR) approach. The Committee stated that:

> a weighted risk ratio in which capital is related to different categories of asset or off-balance sheet exposure, weighted according to broad categories of relative riskiness, is the preferred method for assessing the capital adequacy of banks. (BIS, 1988, paragraph 9)

The RAR is a comparatively simple approach, it sets out to appraise capital adequacy on the basis of banks' relative riskiness. Banks' assets are divided by the supervisory authorities into a number of equivalent risk classes. Different 'risk weights' are assigned to each of the equivalent risk classes of assets. (Risk weights are not considered to be absolute measures, they merely reflect relative riskiness across asset types.) Total weighted risk assets and the RAR are calculated as follows:

$$1. \quad W = \sum a_i r_i \qquad \text{where} \quad A = \sum a_i$$

and

$$2. \quad \text{RAR} = C/W$$

W = total weighted assets
RAR = risk-assets ratio
A = total bank assets
a_i = risk classes of assets
r_i = risk weights
C = capital as defined by the supervisory authorities

(*Note*: risk asset weightings can also be assigned to off-balance sheet items)

If the RAR calculated by the bank falls below the minimum ratio stipulated by the regulatory authorities then this obviously indicates the institution has inadequate capital.

In the Basle proposals the framework of risk weights has been kept as simple as possible and only five weightings are used: 0, 10, 20, 50 and 100 per cent. Assets are assigned into categories of relative riskiness according to their deemed credit risk exposure because this is the major type of risk for most banks. (Credit risk refers to the risk of counterparty failure, for example, the failure to repay a loan as it falls due.) Risk asset weightings are applied to both on and off- balance sheet items. The weighting structure of the RAR scheme is set out in Annexes 2 and 3 of the BIS (1988) paper. The only on-balance sheet assets that carry a 0 per cent weight are:

1. cash,
2. claims on central government and central banks denominated in national currency and funded in that currency,
3. other claims on OECD central governments and central banks,
4. claims collateralised by cash on OECD central governments.

Just to illustrate other weightings, interbank deposits with a maturity of less than one year have a 20 per cent weighting, mortgages have a 50 per cent weighting and claims on the private sector have a 100 per cent weighting. (The case of off-balance sheet items is more complex. Credit risk on these exposures are calculated by applying credit conversion factors to different types of instrument or transaction. The credit conversion factors are then multiplied by the weights applicable to the category of the counterparty for an off-balance sheet transaction. For example, standby lines of credit have a 100 per cent conversion factor and once converted would have the same on-balance risk weighting as claims on the private sector at 100 per cent. This means that standby lines of credit have to have 100 per cent capital backing.)

The RAR is calculated by dividing the total weighted assets by capital. The Basle proposals definition of capital is shown in Table 8.1. It can be seen that there are two types of capital, Tier 1 (core capital) and Tier 2 (supplementary capital), the former being the highest quality: ordinary paid-up share capital/common stock and disclosed reserves. Tier 2 capital is limited to a maximum of 100 per cent of the total of Tier 1 elements and subordinated debt is limited to a maximum of 50 per cent of Tier 1 elements. The Committee on Bank Regulations and Supervisory Practices (CBRSP) Basle (1988)

Table 8.1 *The Basle Proposals – Definition of Capital Included in the Capital Base* (to apply at end 1992)

A. **Capital elements**
   Tier 1 (a) Ordinary paid-up share capital/common stock
   (b) Disclosed reserves

   Tier 2 (a) Undisclosed reserves
   (b) Asset revaluation reserves
   (c) General provisions/general loan loss reserves
   (d) Hybrid (debit/equity) capital instruments
   (e) Subordinated term debt

The sum of Tier 1 and Tier 2 elements will be eligible for inclusion in the capital base, subject to the following limits.

B. **Limits and restrictions**

   (i)   The total of Tier 2 (supplementary) elements will be limited to a maximum of 100 per cent of the total of Tier 1 elements;

   (ii) subordinated term debt will be limited to a maximum of 50 per cent of Tier 1 elements;

   (iii) where general provisions/general loan loss reserves include amounts reflecting lower valuations of assets or latent but unidentified losses present in the balance sheet, the amount of such provisions or reserves will be limited to a maximum of 1.25 percentage points, or exceptionally and temporarily up to 2.0 percentage points, of risk assets;

   (iv) asset revaluation reserves which take the form of latent gains on unrealised securities (see below) will be subject to a discount of 55 per cent.

C. **Deduction from the capital base**
   From Tier 1: Goodwill
   From total
   Capital: (i) Investments in unconsolidated banking and financial subsidiary companies
   N.B The presumption is that the framework would be applied on a consolidated basis to banking groups.
   (ii) Investments in the capital of other banks and financial institutions (at the discretion of national authorities).

D. **Definition of capital elements**

   (i) **Tier 1:** includes only **permanent shareholders' equity** (issued and fully paid ordinary shares/common stock) and disclosed reserves (created or increased by appropriations of retained earnings or other surplus, e.g. share premiums, retained profit, general reserves and legal reserves). In the case of consolidated accounts, this also includes minority interests in the equity of subsidiaries which are less than wholly owned. This basic definition of capital excludes revaluation reserves and preference shares having the characteristics specified below in (d).

(ii)   **Tier 2:**

(a) **Undisclosed reserves** are eligible for inclusion within supplementary elements provided these reserves are accepted by the supervisor. Such reserves consist of that part of the accumulated after-tax surplus of retained profits which banks in some countries may be permitted to maintain as an undisclosed reserve. Apart from the fact that the reserve is not identified in the published balance sheet, it should have the same high quality and character as a disclosed capital reserve; as such, it should not be encumbered by any provision or other known liability but should be freely and immediately available to meet unforeseen future loss. This definition of disclosed reserves excludes hidden values arising from holdings of securities in the balance sheet at below current market prices (see below).

(b) **Revaluation reserves** arise in two ways. Firstly, in some countries, banks (and other commercial companies) are permitted to revalue fixed assets – normally their own premises, from time to time in line with the change in market values. In some countries the amount of such revaluations are determined by law. Revaluations of this kind are reflected on the face of the balance sheet as a revaluation reserve.

Secondly, where formal revaluations are not permitted, hidden values or 'latent' revaluation reserves may be present. Of particular importance in some banking systems are hidden values relating to long-term holdings of equity securities where the difference between the historic cost book valuation and the current market price may be substantial.

Both types of revaluation reserve may be included in Tier 2 provided that the assets are prudently valued, fully reflecting the possibility of price fluctuation and forced sale. In the case of 'latent' revaluation reserves a discount of 55 per cent will be applied to reflect the potential volatility of this form of unrealised capital and the notional tax charge on it.

(c) **General provision/general loan loss reserves**: provisions or loans loss reserves held against future, presently unidentified losses are freely available to meet losses which subsequently materialise and therefore qualify for inclusion within second-ary elements. Provisions ascribed to impairment of particular assets or known liabilities should be excluded. Further more, where general provisions/general loan loss reserves include amounts reflecting lower valuations of assets or latent but unidentified losses already present in the balance sheet, the amount of such provisions or reserves eligible for inclusion will be limited to a maximum of 1.25 percentage points, or exceptionally and temporarily up to 2.0 percentage points.

(d) **Hybrid (debt/equity) capital instruments**. This heading includes a range of instruments which combine characteristics of equity capital and of debt. Their precise specifications differ from country to country, but they should meet the following requirements:

- they are unsecured, subordinated and fully paid-up;
- they are not redeemable at the initiative of the holder or without the prior consent of the supervisory authority;
- they are available to participate in losses without the bank being obliged to cease trading (unlike conventional subordinated debt);
- although the capital instrument may carry an obligation to pay interest that cannot permanently be reduced or waived (unlike dividends on ordinary shareholders' equity), it should allow service obligations to be deferred (as with preference shares) where the profitability of the bank would not support payment.

Preference shares, having these characteristics, would be eligible for inclusion: long-term preferred shares in Canada, *titres participatifs* and *titres subordonnés à durée indeterminée* in France, *Genusscheine* in Germany, perpetual subordinated debt and preference shares in the United Kingdom and mandatory convertible debt instructions in the United States. Debt capital instruments which do not meet these criteria may be eligible for inclusion in item (e).

(e) **Subordinated term debt**: includes conventional unsecured subordinated debt capital instruments with a fixed term to maturity and limited life redeemable preference shares. Unlike instruments included in item (d), these instruments are not normally available to participate in the losses of a bank which continues trading. For this reason these instruments will be limited to a maximum of 50 per cent of Tier 1.

Source: Committee of Banking Regulation and Supervisory Practices, Basle (1988)

proposals sets a target standard ratio of capital to weighted risk assets of 8 per cent, of which core capital should be at least 4 per cent. 'This is expressed as a common minimum standard which international banks in member countries would be expected to observe by the end of 1992, thus allowing a transition period for any necessary adjustment by banks who need to build up to those levels' (CBRSP, 1988).

There has also been a European dimension to international bank supervision. Work at Brussels on the development and testing of capital adequacy ratios for banks and other credit institutions started in the late 1970s. The work at Brussels and Basle overlapped to some extent, but there were important differences. Seven of the major EC countries were also members of the Basle Committee. But the work on capital adequacy at Brussels was designed to cover banks and all credit institutions within the EC, and to be legally binding in all EC member states. The focus of the Basle work was on international banking. With the approval of the Second Banking Directive along with the Solvency Ratios and Own Funds Directives, in July 1989, the EC has set its convergence of capital adequacy wheels in motion. Although the proposed EC solvency ratio appears to reflect closely the Basle proposals, practical difficulties are being encountered with the EC's approach to own funds. A significant problem is that many debt and equity hybrids exist in member countries; one example is revaluation reserves. In certain EC countries, revaluation reserves may be converted into equity (Tier 1 capital) through a scrip issue or similar capitalisation process. This is not congruent with the spirit of Basle. Another problem relates to the EC own funds directives which refers to, 'funds for general banking risks'. It is by no means certain what these include and the manner in which these funds should be treated. Despite the problems, however, the adaption of the three aforementioned EC directives should comprise solid foundations for regulating a common internal market for banking activities. They are an integral part of the target for completing the EC internal market in financial services after 1992.

References and further reading

Committee on Bank Regulations and Supervisory Practices (CBRSP) *(1988) International Convergence of Capital Measurement and Capital Standards*, July (Basle: Bank for International Settlements).

Gardener, E.P.M. and Molyneux, P. (1988) *Structure and Regulation of UK Financial Markets*, IEF Research Papers in Banking and Finance no. 6 (Bangor: UCNW).

Goacher, David J. (1986) *An Introduction to Monetary Economics* (London: Financial Training Ltd).

Struthers, J. and Speight, H. (1986) *Money, Institutions, Theory and Policy* (London: Longman).

CHAPTER 9

RECENT TRENDS AND DEVELOPMENTS IN BANKING

INTRODUCTION

This chapter examines the major forces generating change in international banking markets as well as highlighting the current trends and strategic issues facing banks. The first part of this chapter looks at competition, regulation, financial innovation and technological developments whereas the second section deals with issues such as internationalisation and conglomeration.

FORCES GENERATING CHANGE

Competition

During the 1980s three main competitive trends have become apparent:

1. competition has increased between commercial banks,
2. competition has increased between financial institutions,
3. competition has increased in the market for financial services.

The reasons why competition has increased in the retail banking market is because of the changing demographics and financial position of customers. The proportion of the population under 24 years of age is declining within every western developed economy. Amidst the general ageing of populations three groups stand out. The baby boomers born after the Second World War are spending and borrowing to buy houses, raise children and enjoy a higher standard of living than their parents. Those a little older are saving and investing for a retirement. Those over 65 – around 12 per cent of all Americans for instance – are selling their houses and placing the proceeds in income producing investments. These three groups have broadly different financial requirements which all have an impact on the demand for retail services. Individuals are also becoming wealthier. Real incomes per household have increased in most European countries since 1975 and household assets are still growing faster than liabilities. Personal savings as a percentage of disposable income are on a long-term downward trend in the major industrial countries, although personal borrowing is on the increase. Given the changing demography and financial position of the customers, retail demands are becoming more sophisticated and customer loyalty appears to be decreasing. Customers are demanding more services, better information, and most importantly, value for money. In addition, a much wider variety of non-bank financial institutions, as well as non-financial institutions, are entering the retail banking markets. For example, retailing firms such as Marks and Spencer and Sears have introduced storecards that offer a variety of retail products. On the corporate banking side, customers are continually demanding highly specialist products which they expect to pay competitive cost-based charges for. As the largest multinational companies can now enter the financial markets directly, through securitisation and various treasury operations, the demand for traditional banking services from this clientele is expected to decline. Banks are being forced to focus their competitive efforts on the medium to small sized corporate customer.

Over the coming decade, the competitive threat posed to the banks by new entrants in the market for financial services will markedly increase. Building societies, insurance companies, securities firms and other financial intermediaries will create a major impact by offering a broader range of bank related services. Retailers and hire purchase organisations will probably support this invasion. New competition will mainly come from already established domestic firms although with the advent of 1992 inter-European trade in financial services will no doubt increase. It seems likely that new competitors to the banks will tend to offer a wider variety of retail banking products, which is generally considered to be a more profitable market than that for corporate services. As a result of this increased competition banks will have to adopt a more integrated approach to selling bank services. This will enable them to cross-sell products once the bank-customer relationship is established. Market segmentation, relationship marketing and pricing, and the unbundling of products and services will be critically important if banks are to compete effectively in the market for financial services. Despite these competitive pressures, however, commercial banks will still probably hold a dominant market share in traditional business areas well into the 1990s. This will certainly be the case if strategic planning and product management objectives are accurately applied to reflect the aforementioned trends.

Regulation

Structural developments in banking and new forms of competition and new competitors have been stimulated to varying degrees by the regulatory environment. Regulations and the regulatory environment have always had an important effect on market developments, the evolution of banking and associated banking strategies. The structural deregulation of banking systems (as witnessed in the UK Big Bang and the Building Societies Act 1986 which gave banks and building societies, respectively, the authority to conduct a wider range of business) has helped to stimulate a growing array of new competitors and different forms of competition in banking. The recent political emphasis on laissez faire economic policies has also helped promote a more market orientated framework through which financial services can be provided.

A useful distinction to make is between structural regulation and supervisory (or prudential) regulation. Structural regulation is concerned essentially with areas like the kinds of activity permitted by the authorities to different institutions, the establishment of branches and the prices charged by banks and other financial institutions. Supervisory regulation is concerned primarily with controls designed to preserve the liquidity and solvency of banks. In recent years most banking markets have witnessed widespread structural deregulation coupled with supervisory re-regulation.

The current deregulation movement appears to be unstoppable for at least the immediate future. It is a saying that 'dinosaurs do not come back', but heavy structural regulation could return. Financial history suggests that this might be one result of a major, cataclysmic banking crisis or a series of crises in the future. The consensus view, however, is that such crises are not the inevitable result of deregulation and the resultant increased competition that accompanies it. But there is a general view held that inappropriate regulations may be risk-producing and one of the possible causes of crises. The underlying theme of this view is that the market is the actual, or ultimate, deregulator. If supervisory regulations do not recognise or adapt (or re-regulate) according to the forces of the market, market participants will eventually innovate around the regulations. In short, the regulatory agency becomes effectively by-passed through market forces. Some of the resultant innovations and new operations that arise because of lack of regulatory response, however, may fuel increased risk levels within the system.

Recent projected trends in regulation reflect the need for new and sometimes greatly enhanced powers of supervisory regulation alongside structural deregulation (as mentioned in Chapter 8). The signs are that a continuation of these general trends is very likely for at least the immediate (3–5 years forward) and probably near-term (5–10 years forward) future. Continued structural deregulation is likely to be fostered by associated internationalisation and globalisation trends. Some supervisory re-regulation will be needed to ensure that the benefits of increased competition are not secured at excessive costs. These costs include the social costs inherent in periodic banking crises precipitated by possible excessive competition and speculative behaviour. It seems likely that increased supervision will be a part of the likely supervisory re-regulation that is expected. This will be needed to match the pace of innovation, change and increased opportunities for speculative activities that will accompany continued structural deregulation. The main thrusts of expected change, however, will be on improved supervision, new supervisory techniques and greater supervisory co-operation to match developments in the market. This process is already well under way at a European and international level.

There are also other important general forces at work that have a bearing on the future shape and path of banking regulation in Europe and elsewhere. One of the most significant of these is consumerism, and a consequence has been a marked growth in non-industry specific regulation. This kind of regulation is directed specifically at a collection of social goals like consumer protection, discrimination, privacy and disclosure requirements. There are strong indications that this sector of regulatory activity will also grow rapidly during the next decade. Of course, consumer (particularly depositor) protection is itself one important supervisory objective, or rationale.

Financial innovation

Innovation has been a fundamental driving force in the modern development of banking. It is expected to continue as a major force in the future. Innovation may be regarded broadly as the first or early employment of an idea by one (or a group) of institutions. Another view is that innovations covers products that provide a novel or unique experience for bank customers: this view of innovation also encompasses the systems, procedures and instruments that make these products possible. Innovations usually take two forms – product innovations and process innovations – and these may be complementary. A product innovation involves an alteration in the existing parameters of a product or service offered to the market. A process innovation, on the other hand, involves a change in the nature and utilisation of inputs within a specific production process. Process innovations may also be concerned more generally with sustaining and increasing the volumes produced (and sold) of a new product.

Numerous examples of recent product innovations exist in banking: they include instruments like euronote facilities and products like Merrill Lynch's (truly innovative) cash management account. Examples of process innovations in banking include the growth in the proportion of interest-sensitive liabilities in banks' funding structures and the possibly greater leveraging on bank capital associated with the extension of off-balance sheet activities.

There is little doubt that banks have become increasingly aware with respect to change and innovation. A strong consensus exists amongst banks that successful product and service development, together with subsequent marketing, will be important factors for bank profitability during the next decade. As competitive trends intensify, the differences between successful and unsuccessful institutions will become more pronounced and less easy to correct. The ability to innovate and manage associated change will be crucial factors. Innovation at a bank strategic level is concerned with product, operation (or process) and managerial and organisational innovation. These three strategic levels are interrelated.

Product innovation is concerned with identifying, generating and undertaking new banking instruments and services. At a more general level, financial innovation may encompass two different phenomena – new instruments and marked changes in the comparative importance of different channels of intermediation. In reality, these two phenomena are invariably related. Euronote facilities and the securitisation process in international banking are an example; both of these innovations are the product of the same sets of economic stimuli, and both are directly related in an operational sense. Product innovations in this kind of banking market are typically identified and generated by a small handful of innovative banks. Other competitors then simply copy or 'poach' – in the current absence of any copyright legislation on new banking and finance products – these innovations. Competition may lead subsequently to a growing array of 'bells and whistles' on the basic product innovation. Other banks besides the primary innovators may be very active in this particular innovatory phase.

Some product innovations in banking are simply old instruments being repackaged or revamped for the current marketplace. All innovations can be characterised as different proportions of a small number of basic financial characteristics or attributes, like liquidity and risk-transferral (or hedging). In this general sense, no product or service is truly new. As a result, it may be useful sometimes to draw a distinction between invention (or discovery), innovation (introducing the discovery into the market) and diffusion (a subsequent production and consumption of the invention). Invention is relevant in the present context, because the ability to develop new products may be important for bank profitable survival in some market segments. The top end of the international wholesale market may be one example. Nevertheless, for operational purposes it will be more useful to restrict ourselves to the term innovation.

Numerous financial innovations have been developed by banks and other financial institutions in recent years to meet the ever-changing demands of both the retail and corporate bank customer. The main innovations that have taken place are as follows

1. Growth in the use of interest-sensitive funding and liability management.

Both banks and their customers have become much more interest sensitive over recent years. Banks have begun to borrow a larger proportion of their funds through the international money markets. Depositors, on the other hand, have sought to earn better returns on their deposits by placing them with institutions that offer cash management services such as money market mutual funds, high-interest chequing facilities, (savings accounts with chequing facilities, etc.). Because of this increased interest rate sensitivity of customers, banks have had to compete more aggressively for funds with non-bank financial intermediaries. Over the last ten years, the share of interest-bearing instruments in the broadly defined money stock has increased in all OECD countries. In fact, the share of financial instruments with market related interest rates in the broadly defined money stock exceeds 75 per cent in the United Kingdom.

2. Increase in the amount of variable or floating rate debt and maturity shortening.

As a result of interest rate volatility, most banks now lend at variable and/or floating rates of interest. This has been the case for some time in the United Kingdom, but in the United States, where the savings and loan associations have experienced severe difficulties as a result of fixed rate lending, greater emphasis has been placed on variable rate lending. Large corporations that have traditionally raised capital in the fixed-term eurobond markets are now raising variable rate funds through the issue of floating rate notes (FRNs), medium-term notes (MTNs), euronotes and commercial paper. New instruments, such as euronotes, allow the borrower the opportunity to raise long-term funds while issuing a stream of short-term notes. This illustrates the aspect of maturity shortening.

3. The growth of financial markets and marketable financial instruments.

Not only have existing markets expanded and deepened in recent years, but markets in new financial instruments such as options, swaps, futures, commercial paper, etc., have also developed.

The Cross Report (1986) on *Recent Innovations in International Banking* developed a taxonomy of financial innovations based on their main characteristics or functions. The following scheme was devised:

(1) Risk-transferring innovations: these innovations allow economic agents to transfer amongst themselves the price or

credit risks that characterise financial positions, examples of which include, floating rate loans, adjustable rate mortgages, futures, swaps, options.

(2) Liquidity-enhancing innovations: these innovations allow economic agents to improve the liquidity of their assets as well as the financial system as a whole. They include such things as, loan swaps, securitised assets, sweep accounts, money market mutual funds, etc.

(3) Credit-generating innovations: innovations that provide access to new sources of credit, e.g. zero coupon bonds, junk bonds, eurofacilities.

(4) Equity-generating innovations: innovations that provide new forms of ownership contracts such as equity participation financing, debt for equity swaps, etc.

Many of the above financial innovations are what is known as off-balance sheet items. The 1980s has witnessed a massive growth in banks' off-balance sheet business because historically they did not incur any capital backing. 'The off-balance sheet description reflects that the activities involve contingent commitments not captured as assets or liabilities under conventional accounting procedures. A loan enters as an asset on a bank's balance sheet, whereas a promise to make a loan is a contingent liability: it is an obligation to provide funds should the contingent be realised and does not appear on the balance sheet until after that occurrence' (Lewis and Davis, 1987). Off-balance sheet business is sometimes referred to as the 'invisible bank'. Types of off-balance sheet business fall into four main categories; commitments – such as unused overdraft facilities and revolving lines of credit, guarantees – such as standby letters of credit and acceptances, foreign exchange and interest rate related transactions – such as currency and interest rate options and futures contracts, and finally securities underwriting. What distinguishes this type of business from traditional activities is that it is not margin based: income comes predominantly from fees, commission and trading returns.

Technology

The economic impact of new technology depends upon the rate of increase of new technology and its corresponding absorption rate by banks and financial institutions. Present and prospective developments in the technologies associated with the financial services industry suggest a future characterised by possibly dramatic changes. Past experience with technology absorptions in banking, however, might not by itself wholly support this more dramatic perspective. There has been an apparent gap between potentially available (or prospective) technologies and operationalised (or utilised) technologies in banking. Nevertheless, the rate of absorption has still been impressive, and there are grounds for expecting that this absorption rate will accelerate. Technology, innovation and competition represent a confluence of forces that signal an era that is already producing major unprecedented changes and new challenges for banking. A brief survey of payments systems in Europe during the past five years suggests that there has been comparatively few recent dramatic changes in electronic banking. The most obvious changes have been in the large increase in the number of ATMs (automated teller machines) throughout the United Kingdom and Europe. As you should already be aware ATMs are computer-linked terminals which can be located either on or off bank premises to perform several basic teller functions. Services typically include receiving deposits, transferring funds between accounts and dispensing funds. The popularity of ATMs rests on two main facts: first they remove the necessity to employ costly bank staff, and secondly, they can be accessed 24 hours a day, if outside bank premises. The number of ATMs in Europe has risen from zero in 1967 to approximately 45 000 in 1987.

Many countries have also conducted EFTPOS (electronic funds transfer at point of sale) and home banking experiments. EFTPOS is a means by which payment may be made for goods at the point of sale via computer linked terminals. Bank customers are issued with magnetically striped cards (similar to cash point cards) known as debit cards. These cards are used in the special point of sale terminals of retailers or other organisations; the terminals being connected to the retailer's bank computer. When a customer makes a purchase, he or she requests a transfer of funds by inserting their card into the terminal and entering his or her personal identification number. The sales clerk enters the amount of the transaction, and the terminal requests the customer's depository institution to authorise a transfer. The customer's funds are verified, and, if sufficient, the transfer is authorised, and the amount is immediately credited to the retailer's account. If the customer's account is different to the retailers, a central switching system is used to route and direct the electronic message. In this case where the transfer of funds is immediate, the system is known as 'on-line'.

To date, electronic funds transfer at the point of sale (EFTPOS) and Home and Office Banking (HOB) are not as well established as ATM networks. (Some of these issues have already been discussed in Chapter 6.) The majority of experiments and systems that are being developed and tested involve connecting a retailer's cash register so that electronic messages can be transmitted to the bank. France currently leads the world in electronic banking. In fact, French banks are committed, with the government, to one national system for electronic funds transfer based on the chip (or smart) card by 1990. Nearly two-thirds of the 65 000 French EFTPOS terminals are bank-owned while the remainder are owned by retailers themselves. Two EFTPOS experiments are already underway in the United Kingdom; Counterplus, run by Clydesdale Bank in Scotland and confined mainly to petrol stations, and Speedline, centred on Milton Keynes, run by Midland Bank.

As already mentioned elsewhere in this book Home and Office Banking Systems (HOBS) enable customers to access their bank accounts via a home or office computer linked to their bank's mainframe computer. Balance enquiries, fund transfers, bill payment, insurance payments and the like can be initiated with the use of a TV screen, personal computer or variable tone, push button telephone, depending on the systems available. In the United Kingdom, the Nottingham Building Society was one of the forerunners of home banking. Recently, the TSB has introduced a home banking system. Experiments with HOB systems are more advanced in some countries than in others, but, maybe with the exception of various corporate cash management services, a sophisticated HOBS offering a broad range of services on a national scale has not yet developed.

Table 9.1 summarises the major landmarks in the development of banking technology up to the present; it illustrates the contemporary importance of technology to banks. Individual countries have moved along the path at different rates and, sometimes, in different ways. These trends reflect those factors unique to individual countries – examples include the different economic, political, social and institutional structures of countries. Originally, banks employed computers and associated technology to cut their costs. We are now into an era when IT is increasingly being used by banks to develop, produce, manage and deliver new products and services. Other contemporary developments are expected to accelerate the impact and absorption of technology into banks and other financial sector institutions.

Table 9.1 *Banking Services Based on Electronic Technology[1]*

System	Installation date of early systems
Accounting	1958–65
Voucher (cheque or giro form) sorting for clearings	1963–68
Branch on-line data collection	1965–75
Cash dispensing machines	1966–71
Automated clearings (EFT)	1968–73
Teller counter terminal systems for transaction processing	1971–76
ATM systems for cash dispensing and self-service banking	1972–76
Terminal systems for non-cash self-service banking	1977–80
EFTPOS systems for transactions	1980–present
Home banking systems for self-service banking	1980–present
Branch information systems	1982–present

Note: [1] These data were compiled from banks and the general literature and represent installations on a world average. Certain countries were substantially earlier with some systems.

Source: Smith (1984, p. 44, Table 1)

Deregulation, structural change and intensifying competition seem likely to accelerate the diffusion of technology into banking. New concurrent developments in technology – particularly in the communications field – have emphasised the transition from traditional banking to a more generalised and sophisticated financial services industry. The emphasised role of information in financial products allows a growing array of new competitors (including non-banks) into traditional banking markets. It also offers enhanced possibilities for new product development, and the pressures to use information technology in this way will increase with competition.

CURRENT TRENDS AND STRATEGIC ISSUES FACING BANKS

Banking in the United Kingdom is expected to experience marked changes during the coming years as a result of the completion of the EC single market in 1992 and the increasing influence of six main forces; internationalisation, universalisation, securitisation, globalisation, conglomeration and concentration. Some of these issues have been discussed elsewhere in this text, this section aims to discuss them in more detail.

Internationalisation

Internationalisation is exemplified by the substantial increase in the presence of banks and other financial institutions outside their domestic markets. The internationalisation of UK as well as European banking has had three main effects which have led to increases in:

1. the importance of foreign assets and liabilities of domestic banks,
2. the number of foreign institutions operating in domestic banking markets,
3. the assets of foreign banks operating in banking markets.

Recent evidence suggests that foreign banks will increasingly pose a threat in domestic banking markets especially with business relating to large to medium-sized corporate customers and wealthy personal clients. There is also a definite trend towards outsider penetration in these markets, especially when the incumbent domestic banks are perceived as lacking expertise. In Europe over the coming decade only large foreign banks are expected to form the major competitive threat in the retail banking market, so long as opportunities exist and they are able to acquire institutions with large customer bases. Nevertheless, the current trend is for eurocurrency banking business to continue to displace domestic currency banking business in the balance sheets of many European banking sectors.

Universalisation

Banks are also becoming universal in their outlook offering a broader range of products and services. At present various demarcation lines exist limiting various types of institutions to specific lines of business. Throughout Europe banks are now moving towards universal-type banking systems enabling them to operate in markets that were previously restricted. The rapid erosion of traditional distinctions between banking and the provision of other services has also been mirrored by a concurrent erosion of traditional distinctions in international financial markets, especially between bank and bond finance markets. The breakdown of demarcation lines between banking, capital and money markets business will continue to be fuelled by the securitisation phenomenon.

Securitisation

At its most basic level, the term securitisation refers to techniques whereby assets are transformed or repackaged into financial assets that can be resold to investors in the capital markets. In the euromarkets securitisation has been associated mainly with the growth and replacement of traditional bank finance in the form of syndicated bank credits (eurocredits or euroloans) by FRNs (floating rate notes), euronote facilities including NIFs (note issuance facilities), RUFs (revolving underwriting facilities), commercial paper and others. The securitisation phenomenon has resulted in banks losing their comparative advantage to securities markets in the intermediation of international credits. The securitisation process has brought with it a substantial change in the role of the corporate banker. Profitability has now switched from interest margin-based calculations and the emphasis has shifted towards fee income earned on the activities associated with and including the placing of debt instruments with investors.

Globalisation

Globalisation refers to the worldwide integration of both capital and money markets – the global integration of financial markets – through the swaps mechanism and the associated arbitraging of international rate differences. Globalisation has now made it possible for banks and other financial institutions to manage global investment portfolios. A whole range of new financial products and processes are now available which enable market players to operate in different financial markets simultaneously.

Conglomeration

As mentioned in Chapter 2 financial services are expected in the future to be offered by four main types of corporate entity: conglomerates; specialists; agents and franchisers; groups and associations. Conglomeration is probably the most important of these trends applicable to European banking. The conglomeration movement is characterised by the desire of the larger banks to maintain a global presence as well as offer a universal range of bank products and services. At the present time only a few European countries; Germany, Luxembourg, Spain, Switzerland and the United Kingdom do not apply specific restrictions on the interests of commercial banks in other corporate entities and as such it seems likely that conglomeration will be a more important phenomenon in these countries. A large number of mergers and takeovers in the European financial services marketplace have taken place since 1986. The overriding reasons as to why these have taken place relate to strategic motives associated with diversification and economic motives relating to synergy and growth. Merger and acquisition strategy for banks does not differ from that of other industrial companies despite the fact that they are generally more heavily regulated. One reason why companies invest abroad is because the home market is so saturated. This is particularly relevant to German banks, where over 90 per cent of the population have some form of bank account and the market is considered to be overbanked. The strategic motives for UK and other EC banks expanding overseas have usually been rationalised in terms of diversification and 'follow-the-customer' arguments. The conglo-merate trend will no doubt continue as long as larger institutions wish to expand their multi-product and geographical coverage and as long as the predators have sufficient excess capital to swallow their victims. Partnerships and cross-shareholdings in the financial services marketplace are now widely being used as either insurance policies against the threat of takeover or as a prelude to a possible full merger. Several large Scandinavian banks have recently forged defensive links through cross-shareholdings. The main impetus towards a conglomerate trend has been the perceived growth in importance of investment banking and securities markets activities.

Table 9.2   *Assets and Deposits Concentration Measures*

		Assets concentration measure		Deposits concentration measure	
		5-bank	3-bank	5-bank	3-bank
Germany	1986	.3077	.2079	.2216	.1653
	1985	.3155	.2117	.2323	.1731
	1984	.3220	.2142	.2364	.1783
	1983	.3192	.2103	.2344	.1769
UK	1986	.3235	.2350	.2997	.2163
	1985	.3524	.2510	.3317	.2417
	1984	.3585	.2632	.3374	.2494
	1983	.3875	.2809	.3667	.2674
Japan	1986	.3978	.2482	.4821	.3005
	1985	.3855	.2393	.4642	.2878
	1984	.3920	.2409	.4675	.2865
	1983	.3866	.2383	.4580	.2816
France	1986	.5999	.3933	.6062	.3971
	1985	.6336	.4203	.6335	.4163
	1984	.6393	.4140	.5160	.4036
	1983	.6378	.4139	.6257	.4024

Note: Calculated using International Bank Credit Analysis Ltd (IBCA) database. These estimates provide the same ranking of concentration as in Table 12.1 but the figures are not identical because the IBCA bank data and market size figures are calculated on a different basis.

Source: McLeay and Molyneux (1989)

Concentration

The concentration of banking markets has also been an important feature of structural change. Concentration is by no means a recent phenomenon and many countries' banking systems have been dominated by a handful of large banks, for at least half a century or so. Banking systems differ in their competitive degree of concentration. The three- and five-bank ratios are the most common tools used to measure concentration. The three- and five-bank ratios calculate the proportion of banking sector assets or deposits controlled by the three and five largest banks. Table 9.2 illustrates the degree of banking market concentration in four countries, Germany, United Kingdom, Japan and France. It can be seen from the table that in 1986 France had the most concentrated banking market with the top five banks controlling 59.99 per cent of total banking sector assets and 60.62 per cent of total banking sector deposits. Conversely, the German market appears the least concentrated. From a general perspective, it is difficult to appraise accurately either the efficacy, or extent, of increased concentration within individual banking systems.

It is also becoming much more difficult to measure concentration by contemporary measures, because of the blurring of demarcation lines between banking and other financial markets. It is clear, however, that there appears to be a current preference for larger size in many banks within the United Kingdom and other countries.

References and further reading

Bank for International Settlements (1986) *Recent Innovations in International Banking*, April (Basle: BIS).

McLeay, Stuart and Molyneux, Philip (1989) 'Bank profitability and structure in France, the United Kingdom, West Germany and Japan. Some preliminary findings', *IEF Research Papers in Banking and Finance* RP 89/12 (Bangor: Institute of European Finance).

Revell, J.R.S. (1985) 'New forms of competition and new competitors', *Revue de la Banque*, February, vol. 2, pp. 45–53.

Revell, J.R.S. (1987) *Concentration and Mergers in Banking*, IEF Research Monographs in Banking and Finance, no. 2 (Bangor: UCNW).

Smith, S.P. (1984) *Retail banking in the 1990s: the technology suppliers view* (London: Lafferty).

CHAPTER 10

MONEY MARKETS AND INTERNATIONAL BANKING

INTRODUCTION

The following chapter reviews the functioning of the London discount market, the parallel markets and the eurocurrency markets. It also provides an introduction to the major characteristics and important issues relating to international banking.

LONDON STERLING MONEY MARKETS

Characteristics of money market activities

Money market activities relate to the borrowing and lending of short-term wholesale funds. In general, the maturity of funds varies from overnight to one year. Transactions may take place either on the basis of straightforward borrowing or lending or through the medium of issues of short-term securities. Money markets are intangible in the sense that there is no physical marketplace, unlike for example the London Stock Exchange (before March 1987) where almost all securities transactions took place on the floor of the exchange. Quite simply, the institutions participating in the money markets are brought into contact via sophisticated communications networks, involving telex, telephone and computer links.

The London money markets

It is possible to classify the London money markets according to the nature of their activities. The discount market is the oldest London money market and its origins date back to the early nineteenth century. The parallel (or secondary) sterling money markets evolved from the mid-1950s onwards. Nowadays there are various parallel sterling money markets (the last two in the list are technically not sterling money markets but they act as close substitutes to the traditional markets):

1. treasury bill market,
2. local authority market,
3. sterling acceptance market,
4. inter-bank market,
5. sterling certificates of deposit market,
6. sterling commercial paper market,
7. medium term notes market,
8. floating rate notes market.

The discount market

At the beginning of the nineteenth century banks began to buy and sell bills from each other as a way of managing their short-term liquidity positions. At the same time specialist institutions, now known as discount houses, evolved which concentrated on bill brokerage activities. The importance of this bill broking market increased as the UK financial system became more sophisticated. The traditional function of a discount house is to purchase bills of exchange and hold them, that is, to finance bills. In recent years, however, the main function of the discount houses has been to discount and hold bills with funds borrowed at call from the banks, and these may then be rediscounted with the banks or central bank.

In addition to the discount houses, the other major operators in the market are the clearing banks, the accepting houses and the Banking Department of the Bank of England. 'Only bills of the highest quality are traded in the discount market and so the acceptance activity is a crucial aspect of the market processes' (Goacher, 1986). Accepting houses, members of the Accepting Houses Committee, form the top echelon of the merchant banking sector. By the beginning of 1986 there were 16 members. These banks have a special relationship with the central banking authorities in that their sterling acceptances are eligible for rediscount at the Bank of England. This is sometimes referred to as eligible paper. The Bank of England's role in the discount market is primarily to issue Treasury bills, by tender on a weekly basis, to buy and sell short-term instruments in respect of its own portfolios and to act as lender-of-last-resort in the market. The main functions of the discount market according to Goacher (1986) are as follows:

1. The market provides a useful pool of liquidity for the commercial banks. A very large proportion of the discount houses' funds comes from the clearing banks on a call or overnight basis, and thus, by rolling over or calling in loans, the banks are able to adjust their liquidity positions.
2. The discount houses act as intermediaries between the Bank of England and the commercial banks. Today, the Bank of England usually buys or sells bills from or to the discount houses as a means of adjusting the level of liquidity within the financial system. The Bank may also operate directly through the discount houses when wishing to lend directly to the banking sector. Clearly, the terms upon which the Bank is willing to deal with the discount houses will be crucial to the ultimate effects of intervention not only on short-term interest rates, but also on the level and structure of interest rates in general.
3. The market provides an important source of short-term finance for the companies via the discounting of commercial bills.
4. The discount houses underwrite the weekly Treasury bill tender, standing ready to purchase any bills not taken up through the competitive bidding process which has existed since 1971.
5. The discount houses also maintain the secondary market in banks' certificates of deposit, and they are also important participants in the markets for short-dated gilt-edged securities and local authority bills.

During the 1970s the growth of the parallel interbank sterling money market reduced the relative importance of the discount market as a way for banks to adjust their liquidity positions. Banks increasingly deposited and raised their funds through the interbank markets rather than holding money at call and short notice with the discount houses.

The parallel sterling money markets

The parallel money markets emerged during the mid-1950s, 'with their growth being encouraged initially by changes in the official financing arrangements for UK local authorities and subsequently by severe credit restrictions applied to the UK clearing banks. Basically, financial institutions which were not restricted by official credit controls sought to create new means of borrowing and lending short-term funds on a wholesale level' (Goacher, 1986). The main difference between parallel market and discount market transactions is that parallel market transactions are all unsecured and there is no lender-of-last-resort facility. Table 10.1 shows the important features of sterling money market instruments.

Treasury bill market
Treasury bills are issued by the Bank of England on behalf of the UK government as a source of short-term funds and as a means of influencing interest rates and liquidity in the money market. They have a maturity of up to 91 days. The central bank undertakes to buy Treasury bills on days of money market shortage thus acting as the lender-of-last-resort. The main features of these instruments are shown in Table 10.1. Intervention in this market is one of the most important tools of short-term monetary policy management.

Local authority market
This market is the longest established of the parallel sterling money markets, 'originating in 1955 when the Public Works Loan Board drew back from being the main source of borrowed funds for UK local authorities' (Goacher, 1986). In fact the Board became something of a lender of last resort. After 1955 the local authorities became an important force in money market activities. Loans to local authorities that comprise the local authority (money) market are of less than one-year duration and may be in one of three forms: bank overdrafts, bill finance or deposits. In fact, the local authorities borrow comparatively little by overdraft and the majority of their short-term funds comes from deposits. Local authorities of a certain size are allowed to issue bills in maturities of between three and six months and these are popular money market instruments as they count as eligible paper at the Bank of England.

Table 10.1 *Important Features of Sterling Money Market Instruments*

Instrument	Issuer(s)	Maturity	Denominations	Quotation	Yield levels	Status
UK Treasury bills	Bank of England	usually 91 days occasionally shorter (typically 1–2 days)	minimum of £50,000 in multiples of £5,000	discount yield basis	generally .25 to .375% below LIBOR	Government guaranteed
Local Authority bills	local authorities	usually 91 days occasionally 182 days	usually £5,000; £10,000; £25,000; £50,000 or £100,000	discount yield basis	slightly higher than T-bills	not government guaranteed but considered highly secure
Sterling acceptances	corporations	predominantly 91 days maximum 182 days	normally £25,000 to £1,000,000 – can be smaller	discount yield basis	eligible – .25 to .185%. Ineligible – typically 0.125% higher. Trade bills highest of all commercial bills	eligible-most secure, trade bills-least secure
Deposits Call deposit	UK clearing banks, commercial banks, foreign banks in London, accepting houses and building societies	overnight or 7 days	minimum £50,000 (more marketable at £1m in overnight market)	Simple interest yield	LIBID	Senior debt of the issuer
Time deposit	as above	7 days or 1,2,3,6 & 12 months		Simple interest yield	LIBID	as above
Certificates of deposit	as above	3 months to 5 years – rare beyond 1 year	usually from £50,000 to £500,000 in steps of £10,000	fixed coupon issued at par	between 0.0625 and .25% below LIBID depending on maturity	as above
Sterling Commercial paper	corporations with net assets of £25m or more and listed on the Stock Exchange	between 7 days and 5 years	minimum of £100,000	discount yield basis	typically between LIBID and LIMEAN, though some lesser names at a few bp below LIBOR	

Source: *The Treasurer*, March 1989, and own updates on the sterling commercial paper market

The majority of local authority short-term finance, however, comes from large denomination deposits at terms ranging from overnight at call, to seven day notice to terms up to 364 days. The majority are for 91 days. Brokers arrange these loans and they are usually denominated in multiples of £50 000. The interest rates paid on these deposits change from day-to-day, depending on market demand and supply factors. Lenders of these deposits raise deposit receipts which are not tradeable, because there is no secondary market. A lot of these deposits come from overseas. Some come in straight as sterling denominated deposits whereas others may be borrowed in the eurocurrency markets and swapped into sterling.

Sterling acceptance market
The sterling acceptance market (or commercial bill market as it is sometimes known) is a market in time drafts drawn by one corporation or trader on another in order to finance some trading activity. Typically they have 91 day maturities. There are three main types of sterling acceptance; eligible bills, ineligible bills and trade bills. Eligible bills are commercial bills that have been accepted by a bank which is on a list of banks approved by the Bank of England, and subsequently these types of bills are regarded as the most secure and marketable. They are also the most liquid form of sterling acceptance. Ineligible bills, bills accepted by banks not on the approved list, are predominantly traded by the discount houses. Trade bills are regarded as the lowest credit quality type of acceptance and therefore they offer the highest yields, there also tend to be a less liquid secondary market in these instruments.

Sterling interbank market
The sterling interbank market is by far the largest of the sterling parallel money markets. On this market, banks borrow and lend wholesale sums amongst themselves. The transactions are usually in amounts of £500 000 and above. Loans of up to £20 million have been made in this market although £2 million is considered the norm. All loans are unsecured. Operations in the market have developed concurrently with the trend towards balance-sheet management and liability management in particular. This is when banks take wholesale funds in order to bolster their liquidity requirements as well as to make wholesale loans. 'The interest rates established by the interbank market are watched particularly closely

by the banking community, as they are thought to provide a good indication of the marginal cost of funds to banks in general. The key rate in this context is the three-month London Interbank Offered Rate (LIBOR)' (Goacher, 1986). This is the rate at which banks offer to lend funds in the interbank market. (You may also come across LIBID which is the London Interbank Bid Rate. This is the rate which a bank is willing to pay for funds in the interbank market.) LIBOR is taken as a crucial indication of market trends.

Other markets
London has a significant certificates of deposit (CDs) market which is one of the most active and largest sectors in the London money market. The main issuers of CDs are the UK clearing banks, foreign banks, accepting houses and building societies. CD issues made by the five largest clearing banks are considered to be the highest quality and therefore trade at the highest yield. (There is also a well-established foreign currency – mainly yen and dollar – CD market in London.)

A recently developed market has been the sterling commercial paper (SCP) market which became operational on 20 May 1986 and by early June of the same year borrowing programmes totalling £1.7 billion had been announced by 14 companies. There were 150 SCP programmes which had been announced by mid-1989, totalling £13 billion with almost £4 billion in issue. SCP issues have an original maturity of between seven days and five years with the majority issued at maturities between 15 and 45 days. SCP is a collective name for short-term unsecured notes issued by corporate borrowers. The progress of this market since its inception has been steady, although changes introduced in the 1989 Budget (discussed in Chapter 1) aim to promote growth in this market.

In addition to all the above there has recently grown up a number of markets in closely competing instruments, such as medium-term notes (MTNs) and floating rate notes (FRNs). MTNs are corporate debt instruments which are available at a range of maturities, in fact, the fixed rate MTN is very similar to SCP but has a longer maturity spectrum. FRNs are medium-term debt securities that pay floating rate coupons. There are many MTN and FRN derivative products that are currently available in the United Kingdom which also closely compete with longer-term traditional money-market instruments.

THE EUROCURRENCY MARKETS

Historical development

You can gain a clearer understanding of what we mean by the term 'Eurocurrency market' by abstracting back to the forerunner of the markets – the emergence of the eurodollar market in the 1950s. Eurodollars are defined as US dollars held with banks located outside the USA, including dollar deposits in overseas branches of US banks. Since eurodollars are exactly the same as dollars held in the United States, they are interchangeable with each other. Despite the prefix 'euro', eurodollars can be held by banks anywhere in the world outside the United States, not just in Europe.

Eurodollars are created when an owner of a dollar deposit with a bank in the United States transfers that deposit to a bank or individual outside the United States. The accepting bank abroad receives, in settlement of the transaction, a dollar balance with a bank in the United States. In the case of this transaction, then, ownership of the dollar deposit in the United States is acquired by the financial institution or individual abroad and is off-set by that institution's assumption of a deposit liability payment in US dollars. However, the total of bank deposits in the United States remains unchanged, while an additional dollar deposit has been created abroad. This is why Milton Friedman once stated that the source of eurodollars is a bookkeeper's pen!

The concept of eurocurrencies is exactly the same as that of eurodollars. Eurocurrencies are deposit liabilities held with banks in a currency other than the currency of that bank's country.

There are two necessary conditions for a bank deposit to be termed eurocurrency:

1. the receiver of the deposit must be a banking institution,
2. the banking institution receiving the deposit must be located outside the eurocurrency's country of origin.

Banks that accept eurocurrency deposits are called eurobanks. A eurobank is not a unique institution. Most banks accept eurocurrency deposits and hence, most banks can be referred to as eurobanks. However, because most countries treat domestic and foreign currency transactions differently, 'eurobanking' is generally exempted from strict domestic banking regulations. This has, undoubtedly been a major reason for the rapid post-war development of eurobanking activities.

Most euromarket experts believe that the eurodollar market originated in 1957, when the UK government banned the use of sterling in trade credits between non-residents because of speculative attacks on sterling after the 1956 Suez Crisis. The most obvious alternative to sterling was the US dollar and so British and other international banks sought to use the dollar in trade credits where sterling was restricted.

Some market experts, however, would place the birth of the eurodollar market as far back as the period of the Cold War in the late 1940s and early 1950s. This argument states that in 1949 the new Chinese communist government, fearing an American freeze on its dollar deposits held in the US, began to move these deposits from banks in the United States to the Russian owned Banque Commerciale pour l'Europe du Nord in Paris, and the Moscow Narodny Bank in London. It was not long before other Eastern European countries followed suit, giving birth to foreign dollar deposits in Europe.

Furthermore, the substantial US balance of payments deficits experienced periodically since the early 1960s have placed dollar denominated financial claims into the hands of overseas residents and have thus encouraged the holding of eurodollar deposits.

For many years, the operation of 'Regulation Q' in the United States, (which set maximum permissible interest rates payable on US bank deposits) served to heighten the interest rate advantage attainable by placing dollars on the eurodollar market rather than depositing them with banks in the USA which paid artificially low rates of interest. In addition, to the extent that US banks were unable to bid for funds, their ability to make dollar loans was constrained, and this too encouraged US companies to seek funds overseas.

Also, between 1964 and 1974, an interest equalisation tax operated in the USA. This tax was intended to dissuade foreign residents from taking advantage of low rates of interest charged on dollar loans within the USA. Once again, activities in the eurodollar market can only have benefited from this restriction on US domestic financial activities.

The growth of the eurocurrency activities has been almost continual since the early 1960s, with only two significant periods of interruption to the trend. The first period was in the aftermath of the Bankhaus Herstatt collapse in West Germany during 1974. The second period of somewhat more substantial retrenchment began to appear during the latter half of 1982 and, at least through to 1986, the total volume of eurocurrency activities was virtually stable. The international debt repayments crises, affecting the disturbingly large number of developing and newly developed countries, are thought to have been a major cause of the markets losing their former momentum. The threat that sovereign states might renege on their debt commitments has emphasised the high level of vulnerability of unsecured funds lent internationally, and banks have therefore become much more wary of involvement in certain areas of eurocurrency market activities.

In recent years, both the supply of funds to, and the demand for funds from, the eurocurrency markets has been affected by fundamental changes in world economic conditions. The significant reductions in both the demand for and price of crude oil since 1981 have placed severe financial pressures on a number of the worlds major oil-exporting countries, and this has led to a drying up of the former massive flows of funds to the eurocurrency markets from these nations. On the demand side, the general world recession and the historically high interest rates have tended to dampen the requirements for borrowed funds both for international investment and for trading purposes. Massive capital surpluses have appeared in Japan. Unlike their Western counterparts, however, Japanese savers prefer to invest their money in insurance companies and pension funds which in turn creates a massive demand for securities. (This has, undoubtedly provided an impetus to the growth of the eurobond market in recent years.)

Nature of the eurocurrency markets

The main features of the eurocurrency markets are as follows:

1. All transactions are wholesale, usually a minimum of US $1 million (or the equivalent in another currency).
2. Funds are unsecured and usually have a maturity of one year or less. Funds that are lent for longer than one year are usually raised through the issuance of eurocredits (medium term) or eurobonds (longer term).

3. The majority of eurocurrency transactions (78 per cent in December 1985) are denominated in eurodollars with the remainder being denominated by euro-Deutschemarks, euro-Swiss francs, euro-Japanese yen, euro-French francs and euro-sterling.

4. London had a share of just over 30 per cent of overall eurocurrency business at the end of 1985. Since 1977, however, London's relative position as the main centre for eurocurrency operations has declined somewhat *vis-à-vis* the growth of New York and Tokyo.

5. Banks in the eurocurrency market have three types of customer, non-banks, central banks and other commercial banks. Central banks are much more important depositors than borrowers from the market. The opposite is the case for the non-banks. Overall, however, approximately 70 per cent of transactions are done between banks.

6. Eurocurrencies can be viewed as the 'oil that lubricates the wheels' of the euromarkets. The euromarkets consist of financial instruments, euro-equities, eurocommercial paper, eurobonds and swaps, which are bought and sold with eurocurrencies.

A note on the development of the eurobond market

While the eurodollar market is an international money market primarily concerned with short-term credit flows, the eurobond market is an international capital market dealing with long-term bonds. Just as the eurodollar market was created in 1957 due to the British government's restrictions on the use of sterling for trade credits between non-residents, so the eurobond market was created in 1963 due to the US governments introduction of the Interest Equalisation Tax, which discouraged foreign bond issues in the United States' capital market. However, no other national capital market was big enough at that time to accommodate the huge demand for funds by international borrowers. The eurobond market was created in 1963 in response to this need for an international capital market where long-term bond issues could be floated by international borrowers for a worldwide investor clientele.

International bonds are commonly divided into foreign bonds and eurobonds. Foreign bonds are bonds issued by a foreign borrower in a national capital market, underwritten by a national banking syndicate in accordance with the securities laws of the market country and denominated in the currency of that country.

In contrast, eurobonds are bonds issued in the inter-national euromarkets, underwritten by an international banking syndicate not subject to any one country's securities laws, and denominated in any currency.

Regulation of the eurocurrency markets

It is generally agreed that the risks related to lending within the eurocurrency markets are greater than those faced in comparable domestic markets. The fact that funds are unsecured and that the markets do not enjoy support of official lender-of-last-resort facilities are clearly of importance in this respect. Also, activities often involve the establishment of complex chains of intra-market on-lending, making it difficult for banks to establish the level of exposure to risk incurred with any particular transaction. It may be the case that because of falling profits and narrowing margins, banks may discover, to their peril, that their liquidity and capital bases are inadequate to cope with defaults that may occur.

It is also believed that the activities of these markets might have detrimental effects on the operation and effectiveness of national macroeconomic policies. There are three major areas where problems may well arise:

1. The ability of domestic residents to obtain funds within the eurocurrency markets might very easily frustrate the operation of domestic monetary controls. For example, companies might be able to obtain funds for overseas investment and trading purposes in the euromarkets, which will release available domestic sources of funds for the purpose of making domestic expenditure.
2. Whilst the eurocurrency markets provide a useful source of funds for nations experiencing a balance of payments deficit, the markets have, on occasions, lent to nations who have shown little effort to rectify their deficits. As such,

eurocurrency markets may encourage some nations to live beyond their means and so store up problems for the future.
3. The ability of the eurocurrency markets to undertake the international recycling of funds on a truly massive scale, may raise the level of available international liquidity, leading to fears that the markets may stimulate inflationary pressures on a global scale.

The problems which might be generated by the operations of the eurocurrency markets provide obvious reasons why these markets should be brought within some form of regulatory framework. A certain degree of supervision is clearly enacted over the euro-currency markets; however, this supervision which is on a fairly informal level and is co-ordinated through the Bank for International Settlements, certainly does not compare with levels of control operative in most western nations' domestic financial systems. It is often argued that the application of more rigorous controls to the eurocurrency markets might be intended to protect depositors from inexpedient on-lending by market institutions, and borrowers of funds from becoming over-borrowed. Controls might also seek to force banks to take due regard of the need for sufficient capital bases and holdings of liquid assets. However, a more fundamental motivation for controls could be the prevention of 'chain reaction' defaults which might flow over into the domestic banking sectors of host nations.

Whilst it is generally agreed that there may be a good case for control of the markets, it must never be forgotten that the freedom of activities within the markets has been a major case of their successful operation and rapid growth. Any further controls must be flexible in accounting for this fact.

INTERNATIONAL BANKING

International banking is not a new phenomenon, the Florentine banking houses had established an extensive network of offices throughout most of Europe by the fifteenth century. The early Italian bankers also experienced the problems of international debt, with many of them being bankrupted by the default of early English kings. With the rise of nineteenth century empires, particularly those of the French, German and British, there was a rapid spread of international banks into areas of the world where there had previously been no banking system. Today, many of the world's less developed countries, particularly those which are former colonies of the European countries, have banking systems which are dominated by the branches of overseas banks. The major difference between the growth of international banking in earlier years and the growth which has occurred since the early 1960s is the scale of operations. For example, the US bank Citicorp and the British bank, Barclays each have over 2000 branches overseas making them truly global banks.

The activities of present-day international banks can be categorised as follows:

1. accepting deposits and making loans in domestic currency,
2. accepting deposits and making loans in foreign currency,
3. participating in syndicated loans and designing special finance packages for international trade,
4. dealing in foreign exchange,
5. providing payment mechanisms for foreign trade, e.g. money transfer, documentary collections and credits,
6. operating in the new financial markets of options, futures, swaps, etc.,
7. involvement in the eurocurrency markets through eurobond issues, euronote facilities, eurocommercial paper issues,
8. advice and facilities provided for international mergers, acquisitions, investments, etc.

(*See* Lewis and Davis, 1987, *Domestic and International Banking*, ch. 8 (Oxford, Philip Allan) for a more detailed exposition.)

International banking has two main components: foreign banking and eurocurrency banking. We have already discussed eurocurrency banking in the previous section. Foreign banking covers those operations of a bank where the bank deals with a non-resident of the bank's country but conducts its operations in its currency. For example a British bank lending sterling to an American is conducting foreign business. Where a UK bank does not lend sterling but lends an overseas currency to a non-national, then it is conducting eurocurrency business.

The total gross value of international bank lending now probably exceeds $4000 billion ($4 trillion). Of this total, foreign bank lending (i.e. lending domestic currency to non-nationals) accounts for approximately 17 per cent. This indicates the considerable importance of eurocurrency lending. This in turn partly explains the prominence of international banking centres and their importance in the world's financial system. For example, London is the centre of the eurodollar market. Banks operating in this market are making dollar loans rather than the loans originating from New York. Since the eurodollar market is approximately three-quarters of the total eurocurrency market it shows why London is such an important international financial centre.

Foreign exchange markets

The foreign exchange (FOREX) markets are the world's largest financial markets. It was estimated in 1989 that the turnover in these markets averaged $600 billion per day. Three main financial centres dominate this market, London, New York and Tokyo. The average daily turnover in London is $187 billion; in New York, $129 billion and in Tokyo $115 billion. Since international banks are constantly exchanging one currency for another in order to satisfy their customers' needs, these figures again illustrate why so many international banks have established operations in London (nearly 450 by the end of 1988). The growth of these markets has been equally impressive. The New York FOREX market has grown by 92 per cent since 1983 whilst the Tokyo market has grown over 400 per cent over the same period.

Other features of the market include:

1. In London, only 9 per cent of volume reflects underlying commercial transactions.
2. Generally, for every dollar of world trade, the FOREX markets trade $25.
3. In London, three-quarters (of turnover) is in the spot market compared to two-thirds in New York. (The spot rate is today's rate at which the contract is agreed although performance will be in two business days' time. A forward rate is where the rate for a contract is agreed today although performance will be at some time in the future.)

4. In London, foreign exchange brokers (as opposed to dealers) account for over 40 per cent of the market. In New York they account for over 50 per cent of the market – an 84 per cent increase over 1983.

5. In London, only 24 banks accounted for more than 1 per cent of turnover each, and only 10 banks accounted for more than 2 per cent of turnover. The top ten banks account for approximately one-third of the market.

6. Less than half a dozen banks maintain a presence across all categories of business. The leading four banks in London are Barclays, Midland, Citibank and Chemical Bank.

Table 10.2 provides a breakdown of the average daily foreign exchange turnover by currency in London, New York and Tokyo. It can be seen that the bulk of business in Tokyo is dollar–yen denominated whereas a much broader range of business is undertaken in London and New York. Note that there is also virtually no cross-currency dealing, virtually all trade is between the dollar and other currencies.

Table 10.2 *Average Daily Foreign Exchange Turnover by Currency in 1986*

	London *(total: $90 bn)*		*New York* *(total: $50 bn)*		*Tokyo* *(total: $48 bn)*	
	$/£	30%	$/DM	34%	$/Y	82%
	$/DM	28%	$/Y	23%	Other	18%
	$/Y	14%	$/L	19%		
	$/SFr	9%	$/SFr	10%		
	$/FFr	4%	$/C$	5%		
	$/Lira	2%	$/Ffr	4%		
	$/C$	2%	$/Guilders	1%		
Cross-currency (mainly L/DM) of ECU	4%					
Other $ trans- actions	7%					

Source: Based on surveys conducted by central banks, March 1986

Why is the market so large?

The market reflects deals for the following:

1. Short-term investment by financial and commercial organisa-
    tions who are arbitraging on interest rate differentials in the
    eurocurrency markets. This means that these organisations
    are switching funds from one currency to another at times
    when the interest rate differential between the two currencies
    is not reflected accurately in the exchange rate between the
    two currencies.
2. Speculation: mainly financial organisations going 'long' or
    'short' to make a capital gain. This is declining in importance
    under pressure from regulators and the dangers of increas-
    ingly volatile markets. If you refer back to the figures given
    for the average daily turnover in the markets you will
    appreciate the potential for huge losses. Adopting speculative
    positions could expose a bank to risking its entire capital to a
    few minutes' trading in the market. This is such a risky
    position to adopt that all banks cover their commitments to
    some extent at the same time they enter into forward
    contracts. In addition, regulators in recent years have
    imposed increasingly more stringent controls on such risk
    exposure.
3. Intervention by central banks: in total this is a very small part
    of the total turnover. But at some times during the day it may
    be very significant. For example, central banks intervene in
    the markets in order to move exchange rates from a rate that
    the authorities are unhappy with (perhaps because it is
    making exports uncompetitive) to a rate which is more likely
    to help them achieve their macroeconomic objectives. Given
    the size of the market you can see that spending even billions
    of dollars may have only a marginal impact on the market
    (and therefore rates). However, at some times during the day
    there is relatively little activity and intervening at that time
    will have a much larger impact than at other times. For
    example, in the early afternoon (GMT) there is usually
    considerable business occurring because New York, Chicago,
    London and Frankfurt are all open. A large sale at this time
    will have less influence on rates than, say from midnight to

early morning (London time) when San Francisco is closing and Hong Kong has not yet opened.

4. The entrance of new market participants with financial liberalisation occurring around the world. This really needs no explanation. The dismantling of barriers in many of the world's financial centres has allowed new institutions to enter the market increasing the level of activity.

5. The volatility of currencies leading to an elaborate sequence of transactions to 'hedge' (cover) risk, all of which boosts turnover, i.e. a single commercial transaction may be reflected in a string of other deals in the currency markets.

International financial centres

There are three major financial centres which now dominate the world's financial system. These are New York, London and Tokyo. Increasingly, international banking is becoming concentrated in these centres and their importance is likely to grow. For example, over a quarter of all international bank lending is conducted in London, 15 per cent in Tokyo and 12 per cent in New York. The only other financial centres which match the importance of these three centres are the various 'offshore' centres such as those in the Caribbean. These are 'booking centres' where deposits and loans are legally placed but transactions are carried out from the head office of a bank, in other words, they are basically 'tax havens'. They account for approximately 17 per cent of international bank lending.

The reasons for the dominance of London, Tokyo and New York are partly financial and partly geographical. The importance of the dollar and the yen, and the size of the US and Japanese banks, has played a large part in establishing the role of New York and Tokyo. These reasons are not so apparent in the case of London.

US banks conduct over a quarter of their international business through their London offices and Japanese banks conduct over 40 per cent. Why should London have become so important? There are several reasons. The first is geographical. As previously mentioned, London is placed in a time zone between Tokyo and New York, allowing 24-hour dealing if an office is maintained in the three centres. Another reason is the concentration of financial skills found in London including insurance services, commodity trading, stockbroking, bond trading and legal services. The last factor is important since in many cases disputes arising in international business are settled in London.

A further factor is the English language. In the same way that airline pilots need a common language around the world to communicate, so conducting international financial transactions needs a common language.

Perhaps the most important factor is the regulatory environment. This has traditionally been informal and pragmatic in the United Kingdom whereas in most other countries it is considerably more restrictive and formalised. A major facet of this approach is the ability to conduct both banking and securities business in London. This is not possible in either New York or Tokyo. Since banks like to be able to service all the financial needs of their corporate clients, this freedom is very important to them. It means, for example, that they can make corporate loans as well as underwriting new issues of stocks and bonds and giving investment advice.

The international debt problem

The international debt problem concerns the ability to repay international loans taken by many of the world's less developed countries. Of course, not all these countries are unable to repay their loans, but unfortunately many of the countries facing the severest problems of repayment are also the largest debtors. For example, Brazil's debt is now over $100 billion and Mexico's is approaching $100 billion. The total indebtedness of the developing countries is over $1000 billion.

It is no longer realistic to believe that all the developing countries will be able to repay their debt. Some countries facing the most difficulties in debt repayment have unilaterally decided to limit their debt servicing to a percentage of their export earnings. In the case of Peru, this is 10 per cent. If some of the larger debtors were to take the same course of action, the effect would be very serious, especially for the US banks. At the end of 1982, the value of loans which Citibank had made to just five countries, Argentina, Brazil, Mexico, Venezuela and Brazil, stood at 175 per cent of its capital. Bank of America had lent 158 per cent of the value of its capital to these countries, Chase Manhattan had lent 154 per cent, and Manufacturers Hanover 263 per cent. Although capital positions have considerably improved since then, the total value of these debts in relation to the capital employed to support it, still represents the largest single risk in the balance sheet of many banks. In many ways the 'overhang' of this debt on the banking system is a microcosm of the business of banking. It illustrates the need for prudent lending practices; it emphasises the role of capital when things go wrong; and it shows how a bank can become exposed if it becomes too involved with just a handful of customers. (Remember the jibe: if I owe the bank £100 and I cannot repay, I've got a problem but if I owe the bank £100 million and I can't repay, the bank's got a problem.) But, perhaps most importantly of all, the debt problem shows that at the end of the day it is the quality of bank management and not new technology or financial products, that determines the ultimate success of a bank.

References and further reading

Goacher, D.J. (1986) *An Introduction to Monetary Economics* (London: Financial Training).

Lewis, M.K. and Davis, K.T. (1987) *Domestic and International Banking* (Oxford: Philip Allan).

Shaw, E.R. (1978) *The London Money Market*, 2nd edn (London: Heinemann).

Struthers, J. and Speight, H. (1986) *Money, Institutions, Theory and Policy* (London: Longman)

CHAPTER 11

EUROPEAN FINANCIAL SERVICES AND 1992

INTRODUCTION

Financial services are an increasingly important sphere of activity within the EC. This sector produces around 7.5 per cent of total EC output (in terms of value added) and also employs over 3 per cent of the Community workforce. Growth in employment in the banking and finance sectors has typically exceeded 10 per cent during the period 1978 to 1985. Given the size and growth of the financial services sector in many European countries during the 1980s it is important that we consider the effects of the 1992 legislative programme. This chapter briefly examines the EC directives and also provides an overview of the benefits that are expected to accrue from completing the internal market in financial services after 1992. (Chapter 12 covers banking in the EC in more detail and analyses the role of large banks up to 1992.)

EC LEGISLATION AND 1992

European financial ministers agreed the final text for the Second Banking Directive on 10 July 1989. This directive paves the way for completion of a single market for the banking sector within the EC. The main aim of this legislation is to harmonise laws and rules for credit institutions so they can set up and operate freely across the EC subject to adequate supervision. The main provisions of the directive are as follows:

1. minimum capital requirements for banks of 5 million ECUs, special provisions are given for smaller banks,

2. provisions for monitoring and vetting of bodies that have substantial bank shareholdings,
3. controls over banks' long-term participation in non-financial companies,
4. principles for granting host countries the right to control bank liquidity,
5. the establishment of a single banking 'passport' to permit activity anywhere in the EC.

The principle of the single banking 'passport' is of particular importance. Once a credit institution is authorised to do banking business by its home supervisor (normally a central bank) it will have a 'passport' to sell its products and services throughout the EC. This principle is also enshrined in the mortgage credit directive (which allows mortgage lenders that can lend in one country to lend in other EC countries without having to be authorised locally) and the investment services directive (which liberalises the provision of investment services within the EC). The Second Banking Directive does not harmonise conduct of business standards and banks that sell a variety of products – such as consumer lending, mortgages, savings – will still have to ensure that they can comply with local host-country consumer protection and other country specific laws. On the other hand, countries are not allowed to make these aforementioned 'public good' laws discriminate against foreign entrants, they have to be applicable to a class of institution.

The Second Banking Directive was passed by the EC Council of Ministers in conjunction with a Solvency Ratio Directive and an Own Funds Directive. This latter legislation aims to ensure that if each country within the Community recognises each other's banking licences, then each must set similar bank licensing standards. As its name suggests, the Solvency Ratio Directive aims to harmonise solvency ratios for credit institutions within the EC. Banks are required to keep shareholders' funds (capital) at not less than 8 per cent of (on- and off-balance sheet) risk weighted assets. The EC sovlency ratio appears to reflect closely the Basle (BIS) proposals, as discussed in Chapter 8, although there are some minor differences. The Own Funds Directive aims to harmonise the definition of capital for credit institutions operating within the EC and is also similar to the BIS proposals. (Note that the BIS definition of own funds and solvency ratios are geared to international banks and therefore are not legally enforceable, whereas EC standards will be.) Given these developments it is hoped that this new set of regulations should make European financial markets substantially more contestable.

> Banks will no longer face the bureaucratic obstacles of obtaining licences in every country in which they wish to operate. More substantively they will not face many of the implicitly protective regulations that have limited their incentives to enter profitable markets – regulations such as those that impose capital requirements on their individual branches, rather than on their operations as a whole. (Davis and Smales, 1989)

Even though the aforementioned legislation has led to talk of a 'single banking licence' and moves towards a European Banking Act, difficulties have arisen relating to the proposed treatment of non-EC banks. The draft directives did not make it clear whether non-EC banks would benefit from the planned single market in financial services, even if they were largely licensed to operate in a Community country. The draft Second Banking Directive suggested that some form of 'reciprocal treatment' rule would be used. This caused serious concerns, especially for US and Japanese banks, which worried that if a strict interpretation of the reciprocity clause was used, a US or Japanese bank wanting to establish in the United Kingdom could be prevented from doing so, for example, by the Portuguese authorities, if Portuguese banks felt they were not getting proper access to the US or Japanese markets. Despite these fears, however, narrow and rigid reciprocity clauses were 'watered' down by the time the Second Banking Directive was agreed in July 1989. This legislation now allows access to the EC on the basis of access (not necessarily equal) by EC banks to third country markets. The EC Commission still retains the right to take retaliatory action against third countries not granting EC banks conditions equal to their domestic banks.

FINANCIAL SERVICES IN THE EC – THE IMPACT OF COMPLETING THE INTERNAL MARKET

Table 11.1 summarises some of the economic features of the main EC financial services sectors. Within the EC as a whole, over 50 per cent of the output of credit and insurance institutions comprises

Table 11.1 *Economic Aspects of the European Financial Services Sector*

Economic dimensions of the financial services sector (1985)[1]

	Gross value-added as a % of GDP[2]	Employment as a % of total employment[3]	Compensation of employees as a % of total for the economy
Belgium	5.7	3.8	6.3
W. Germany	5.4	3.0	4.4
Spain	6.4	2.8	6.7
France	4.3	2.8	3.8
Italy	4.9	1.8	5.6
Luxembourg[4]	14.9	5.7	12.2
Netherlands	5.2	3.7	4.9
United Kingdom	11.8	3.7	8.5
EUR 8[5]	6.4	2.9	6.2

Economic dimensions of the main financial services branches: insurance premiums, bank loans outstanding and stock market capitalisation, as % of GDP

	Insurance premiums[6]	Bank loans[7]	Stock market capitalisation[8]
Belgium	3.9	142[9]	92
West Germany	6.6	139	89
Spain	2.5	99	69
France	4.3	93[9]	85
Italy	2.2	96	75
Luxembourg	3.1	6916	11125
Netherlands	6.1	130	165
United Kingdom	8.1	208	149
EUR 8[10]	5.2	142	116

[1] defined in the narrow sense as credit and insurance institutions
[2] including net interest payment
[3] employees in employment plus the self-employed
[4] 1982
[5] this aggregate accounted for 95% of total Community GDP in 1985
[6] Average 1978–84
[7] 1984
[8] end 1985
[9] 1982
[10] weighted average

Source:　Commission of the European Communities (1988)

intermediate transactions by other industries. Only 20 per cent of
this output is directed towards householders' final uses. It can be
seen from Table 11.1 that Italy has the lowest proportion, 1.8 per
cent, of its total workforce employed in the financial sector whereas
Luxembourg has the highest figure at 5.7 per cent. This table also
shows that the value added as a percentage of GDP contributed by
financial services amounted to a high of 14.9 per cent in
Luxembourg and a low of 4.3 in France. The relative size of
insurance, banking and capital markets is indicated in the second
half of the table, note that the figures for Luxembourg are
somewhat distorted because they include massive international
bank lending (in the bank loans category) and euromarket business
(in the stock market capitalisation category). If we disregard
Luxembourg, because of its special financial centre status, these
figures imply that in 1985 the United Kingdom had the largest
insurance and banking markets in the EC with the second largest
stock market capitalisation. Things have changed somewhat since
1985, however, and by 1988 West Germany had the largest markets
(according to total insurance premiums, banking sector assets and
stockmarket capitalisation) in all three sectors.

The economic analysis of completing the internal market in
financial services after 1992 provides a broad indication of the kinds
of competitive forces that may be released when the internal market
is completed. Table 11.2 summarises the estimated price falls,
hypothesised from completing the internal market, on a standard
set of financial products as reproted by the EC 'Cecchini' study. The
possible gains from 1992 are reflected in the corresponding
differentials between the prices in individual countries compared
to the level at which overall prices are estimated to settle when the
internal market is completed. Although the data are not forecasts
and have been estimated subject to strong (some say unrealistic)
assumptions, they represent a heroic attempt to suggest possible
post-1992 developments. The theoretical, potential price reductions
shown in section 1 of Table 11.2 indicate the different competitive
conditions that exist in the three main financial services sectors for
eight EC countries. Section 2 adjusts the theoretical, potential price
reductions to reflect more accurately expected price falls. It can be
seen that price falls for financial services are expected to be the
largest in Spain, Italy, France and Belgium. Taking the analysis one
step further, the estimated gains from completing the EC internal

market are summarised in Table 11.3. This shows that the estimated gains resulting from the indicative price reduction for financial services will amount to 0.7 per cent of the EC's gross domestic product. The countries that will derive the largest benefit from the expected fall in financial service prices resulting from 1992 will be Spain, Luxembourg, the United Kingdom and Italy.

Table 11.2 *Estimate of Potential Falls in Financial Product Prices as a Result of Completing the Internal Market* (per cent)

	Belguim	West Germany	Spain	France	Italy	Luxembourg	Netherlands	United Kingdom
1. Theoretical, potential price reductions[1]								
Banking	15	33	34	25	18	16	10	18
Insurance	31	10	32	24	51	37	1	4
Securities	52	11	44	23	33	9	18	12
Total	23	25	34	24	29	17	9	13
2. Indicative price reductions[2]								
All financial services								
Range	6–16	5–15	16–26	7–17	9–19	3–13	0–9	2–12
Centre of range	11	10	21	12	14	8	4	7

Notes: [1] These data show the weighted averages of the theoretical potential falls of selected financial product prices.

[2] Indicative price falls are based upon a scaling down of the theoretical potential price reductions, taking into account roughly the extent to which perfectly competitive and integrated conditions will not be attained, plus other information for each financial services sub-sector, such as gross margins and administrative costs as a proportion of total costs.

Source: Commission of the European Communities (1988)

BANKING PRODUCTS AND SERVICES

Tables 11.2 and 11.3 summarised the estimated theoretical and indicative, potential price reductions in the three main EC financial services sectors, Banking, Insurance and Securities. Table 11.4 contains more detailed banking product data, stratified by country, and it can be seen that West Germany, Spain and France are clearly top of this league table in terms of theoretical, potential price reductions when the internal market is completed. This confirms the post-1992 attractions of these three major EC countries.

Table 11.3 *Estimated Gains Resulting from the Indicative Price Reductions for Financial Sectors*

Estimated gains resulting from the indicative price reduction for financial services

	Average indicative price reduction	Direct impact on value-added for financial services		Gain in consumer surplus as a result of average indicative price reduction[1]	
	%	Mn ECU	% of GDP	Mn ECU	% of GDP
Belgium	11	656	0.6	685	0.7
West Germany	10	4442	0.5	4619	0.6
Spain	21	2925	1.4	3189	1.5
France	12	3513	0.5	3683	0.5
Italy	14	3780	0.7	3996	0.7
Luxembourg	8	43	1.2	44	1.2
Netherlands	4	341	0.2	347	0.2
United Kingdom	7	4917	0.8	5051	0.8
EUR	10	20617	0.7	21614	0.7

Note: [1] Based on the assumption that the elasticity of demand for financial services is 0.75

Source: Commission of the European Communities (1988)

Table 11.4 suggests that one of the biggest competitive impacts of 1992 is likely to be in the retail and middle market segments for financial services. These products (like commercial loans and foreign exchange) show a higher price-reduction potential compared with wholesale financial products. Such results confirm the contemporary, relatively low margins in corporate business. Large companies typically have more bargaining power than individual retail customers, and retail services are less exposed to international competition.

Table 11.4 *Estimate of Potential Falls in Individual Financial Product Prices as a Result of Completing the Internal Market*

	Belgium	West Germany	Spain	France	Italy	Luxembourg	Netherlands	United Kingdom
1. Percentage differences in prices of financial products[1] compared with the average of the four lowest observations[2]								
Banking	%							
Consumer Credit	-41	136	39	105	—[3]	-26	31	121
Credit cards	79	60	26	-30	89	-12	43	16
Mortgages	31	57	118	78	-4	—[3]	-6	-20
Letters of credit	22	-10	59	-7	9	27	17	8
Foreign exchange	6	31	196	56	23	33	-46	16
Travellers cheques	35	-7	30	39	22	-7	33	-7
Commercial loans	-5	6	19	-7	9	6	43	46
2. Theoretical, potential price reductions[2]								
Banking	15	33	34	25	18	16	10	18

Notes: 1. See Table 5.1.3 of Commission of the European Communities (1988) for definitions of the financial products

2. The figures in part 1 of the table show the extent to which financial product prices, in each country, are above a low reference level. Each of these price differences implies a theoretical potential price fall from existing price levels to the low reference level. Part 2 sets down the weighted averages of the theoretical potential falls for each sub-sector.

3. Observations for consumer credit in Italy and mortgages in Luxembourg were not obtained, and have been represented by mechanical estimates in the calculations of the larger aggregates. The data for institutional gilts transactions in the UK were not available on a comparable basis, and so the figures for institutional equity transactions were used in the calculations.

Source: Commission of the European Communities (1988)

As a result, retail services seem to offer the highest potential for price cuts (increased competition) post-1992. For newcomers, retail banking segments correspondingly offer the most attractive expansion opportunities in terms of price-arbitraging possibilities.

Spanish and Italian banks seem likely to experience the highest competitive pressures in terms of theoretical, potential price reductions for all financial services. Table 11.5 summarises the findings of two recent polls of bankers on the attractiveness of European banking systems. It is interesting to note that the United Kingdom, followed by Germany, tops this league table; Spain comes third, followed by Luxembourg, Italy and the Netherlands.

Table 11.5 *Attractiveness of European Markets*

Country	Very attractive	Somewhat attractive	Not attractive
Belgium	21	23	25
Denmark	15	21	32
France	29	25	17
Greece	13	12	36
Germany	55	13	9
Ireland	17	17	30
Italy	28	25	15
Luxembourg	32	22	16
Netherlands	28	18	17
Portugal	15	21	25
Spain	33	19	18
UK	64	8	15

Source: UBS – Phillips & Drew (1988, table 3, p. 87)

The above estimates strongly suggest that competition and resultant cross-border financial activities are likely to increase substantially in the years following 1992. Banks and other financial institutions in retail financial services will increasingly seek to exploit the post-1992 opportunities for trade without establishment.

New delivery systems (like direct mailing) and new associations (such as linking up with intermediaries, like brokers, in other countries) will increasingly be exploited. Successful product and service development and subsequent marketing will be critical strategic factors for all financial institutions. Increasing competition will force banks to become more market-orientated in their strategies. There will be an increasing emphasis on providing customers with the services that they want and not the services that banks believe they should have. Retail banking has traditionally been supply-led, but this is already changing. It is expected that in the run-up to 1992, intensifying competition will encourage banks of all kinds to broaden and improve the quality of their services and customer bases.

One can tentatively predict that in corporate financial services, the larger companies will increasingly use the financial markets instead of traditional bank intermediation. Securitisation will encourage banks to emphasise 'relationship banking', and their competitive ability to deliver banking and related services to these companies. Banks will face a growing adverse selection problem in their lending, and they will be encouraged to concentrate more of their financial resources into middle-and lower-sized companies and venture capital activities. Banks will be much more active users themselves of securitisation techniques during the 1990s. Mortgages and a wide range of other kinds of banking assets, including commercial loans, will be channelled into financial markets off the balance sheets of banks and other financial institutions.

Compared to traditional financial products and services, off-balance sheet (OBS) business will probably increase in importance. In this respect banks will become providers of more insurance-type economic services, like underwriting, and investment banking functions, like arranging and placing new issues. Fee income will increase in importance compared to traditional, interest-margin profits. Together with securitisation, a greater concentration on fee income will enable banks to 'gear up' on their increasingly pressured capital bases. Banks will continue to place a greater emphasis on the unbundling of existing products. A more integrated approach to service provision will facilitate the cross-selling of products once the bank-customer relationship is established.

References and further reading

Bank of England Quarterly Bulletin (1989) 'The single European market: survey of the UK financial services industry', August, pp. 407–12.

Cecchini, P. (1988) *The European Challenge 1992: The Benefits of a Single Market* (Aldershot: Gower).

Commission of the European Communities (1988) 'The economics of 1992', *European Economy*, vol. 35, March (Brussels: EC).

Davis, Evan and Smales, Carol (1989) 'The integration of European financial services' *1992 Myths and Realities*, pp. 91–117, Centre for Business Strategy (London: London Business School).

UBS-Phillips and Drew (1988) *Europe 1992: Breaking Down the Barriers/ Economic and Sector Prospects,* edited by D. Fayil and B. Seward, June (London: UBS-Phillips and Drew).

CHAPTER 12

BANKING IN THE EUROPEAN COMMUNITY AND THE ROLE OF LARGE BANKS UP TO 1992

INTRODUCTION

Probably the most important issue facing European banks over the coming years is how to strategically position themselves in the light of the European Commission's 1992 single market proposals. The following chapter examines EC banking markets and provides an overview of the strategic issues facing banks. It also considers the role of large banks up to 1992.

BANKING IN THE EUROPEAN COMMUNITY

EC banking markets: an overview

Every EC banking market has its distinguishing features, although there are a number of characteristics that help to distinguish continental banking systems from those based on the British model. Revell (1987) identifies five common elements of continental banking systems:

1. the presence of various special credit institutions which are usually publicly owned and provide funds for various sectors such as industry, agriculture and property.
2. the increased importance of savings banks, co-operative banks and co-operative credit associations, together with their central institutions.

3. a long history of commercial banks' participation in the ownership and management of industrial enterprises, 'relics of which still linger on'.
4. the importance in many European countries of banks and other institutions which are organised on a local or regional basis, usually reflecting the prevalence of small enterprises in both industry and agriculture.
5. the similarity between banking laws enacted in most countries after various banking crises at the beginning of the 1930s.

Despite these differences, every banking system in Europe has a group of recognisable dominant or 'core banks', recognised by both the authorities and by the general public which conduct both national and international business. In some EC countries, like France and Spain there has been a trend for the local and regional banks to create groups that could compete effectively with these national 'core banks' in their own regions. Political factors in various countries have also sought to encourage (protect) competition between regional and national banks. In countries with Federal governments, like West Germany, regional institutions play a more important role. In fact, it is still the case that in countries such as France, Italy and Spain, banks are registered at a local, regional and national level. Branching restrictions that remained in many EC countries up until the 1960s (they still remain in Italy) also helped preserve the status quo of various regional and local institutions. Those countries which have a large number of mutual and co-operative banks, such as Germany and France, tend to have a stronger regional focus than countries which have a small number of relatively large private banks.

Table 12.1 provides us with an illustration of the main features of EC banking sectors in 1986. One can see that the concentration measures show that out of the largest four banking sectors in the EC, Italy and France have the most concentrated banking markets. The market power of the 'core' banks in Belgium, Netherlands, Denmark and Ireland also seems to be significant. The figures for the United Kingdom appear diluted because of the inclusion of statistics relating to all the foreign banks based in London.

It is interesting to note that viewing the larger banking sectors, it is those in which regulations are presently most restrictive (France through nationalisation and Italy through branching restrictions and central government ownership) which are the most concentrated. Central government ownership is much more significant in France (around 60 per cent) and Italy (around 40 per cent) than in the other larger banking sectors, although this trend is currently being reversed in France, where banks that were nationalised in 1981 are currently being privatised.

The degree of change in concentration and ownership resulting from the 1992 proposals will be primarily determined by the ability of the larger EC banks to discover and exploit profitable opportunities across countries boundaries.

Table 12.1 *Market Concentration and Size of Banking Sectors in the EC, 1986*

Number of banks in market	Size of banking sector Assets ($ billion)		Concentration % of total market			
			Assets		Deposits	
			5 firm	3 firm	5 firm	3 firm
4465	Germany	1465.0	31.2	21.2	30.5	19.1
661	United Kingdom	1337.8	32.6	26.5	30.3	21.6
367	France	1012.6	63.0	42.3	65.2	45.5
980	Italy	529.2	55.1	35.2	68.5	41.6
349	Spain	332.3	34.7	21.9	38.8	24.3
81	Netherlands	272.3	—	71.3	—	83.9
86	Belgium	228.3	84.7	57.1	87.5	59.0
120	Luxembourg	198.1	22.4	16.7	—	16.5
216	Denmark	111.9	50.9	36.7	58.6	45.3
na	Greece	48.4	—	—	—	49.7
40	Portugal	43.3	—	49.7	—	49.6
43	Ireland	22.1	—	71.0	—	—

Notes: 1. The market size figure for Greece is a deposits figure
2. Sources of information for banking sector size; OECD (1988) and various central bank publications
3. 3 firm and 5 firm concentration ratios calculated using data take from the consolidated accounts published in *The Banker* '500'
4. The number of banks in France increases to around 6000 if mutual associations are included
5. Only 12 of the 120 Luxembourg banks are domestic institutions

Table 12.2 *Structure and Performance Characteristics of the Top Banks in the EC for 1987[1]*
(all figures arithmetic means)

	Number of EC banks in Banker 'Top 500'	Assets $ million	PTP Mean $ million	PTP/ Assets	PTP/ Capital	CAP/ Assets	NINT/ Assets	Employees	Branch networks
Germany	44	33876	161.1	0.47	14.52	3.17	1.57	5555	944
United Kingdom	15	46204	113.0	0.68	7.22	6.44	3.21	31413	1642
France	20	59444	229.5	0.55	15.77	3.40	2.89	19339	1417
Italy	33	25793	200.1	1.08	18.14	5.71	2.73	7009	342
Spain	13	22423	254.5	1.22	22.12	5.86	4.99	11826	1120
Netherlands	5	64772	340.8	0.53	13.77	3.97	2.49	21588	1069
Belgium	9	30420	110.1	0.46	14.69	2.99	2.20	6927	710
Luxembourg	6	10289	66.3	0.57	18.69	3.55	2.46	3973	303
Denmark	8	12904	64.6	0.49	7.63	6.88	3.42	4557	247
Greece	3	14368	45.0	0.52	18.30	2.78	0.66	10388	379
Portugal	4	8612	53.0	0.51	15.52	3.20	2.64	7495	136
Ireland	2	14881	208.0	1.48	24.20	6.13	4.51	9221	239

Note: [1] Figures estimated by author. Data taken from *The Banker* '500' of which 162 banks were EC based banks

[2] **PTP** – pre-tax profits
    CAP – Capital
    NINT – net interest income

THE ROLE OF LARGE BANKS

The structure and performance characteristics of the largest banks in the EC

Table 12.2 provides a detailed analysis of bank structure and performance indicators for the largest banks in the EC. Data has been taken from *The Banker* 'Top 500' which lists the top 500 banks in the world according to US dollar asset size. There are 162 EC banks in the 1987 list. The table is split into three sections to distinguish large, medium and small banking markets. Countries are listed in order of their domestic banking market size. The table provides some interesting insights into the different operational characteristics of top banks and also implicitly suggests features of individual banking systems. The following observations based on mean statistics for 1987 are the most important.

1. French banks are on average, in asset size, the largest in the EC but employ considerable less staff than their UK counterparts.
2. The top UK banks have the largest branch networks and employ considerably more staff than their counterparts in other EC countries. (This could be evidence of some form of non-price competition, possibly expense-preference behaviour.) The average size of branch networks in France and German is overstated by the fact that two central institutions for credit co-operatives, Crédit Agricole (France) and Deutsche Genossenschaftsbank (Germany), conduct business for a large number of credit co-operatives which have 10,153 and 19,500 associated branches respectively.
3. Comparing the relative performance figures for top banks in the large and medium-sized markets we find that Italian and Spanish banks have relatively small average assets size, yet they have the highest pre-tax profit to assets ratio and the highest pre-tax profits to capital ratio. Italian banks have quite small branch networks.
4. The performance figures for the top 44 German banks, 33 Italian banks and 13 Spanish banks are less dispersed than those of the top 15 UK and 20 French banks.

5. The top banks in Germany and France have markedly lower
   capital/assets ratios than banks in the United Kingdom,
   Spain and Italy. Capital/assets figures for German banks are
   much less dispersed than for other banks. Some of these
   points can be explained by: the role of hidden reserves and
   attitudes to loan capital in Germany and the role of the state
   in France.

These statistics indicate why the Spanish and Italian banking
markets appear attractive to large banks from other EC countries.
The above statements may seem rather precarious based on one
year's data but if one considers the same indicators between 1985
and 1987 one arrives at similar conclusions.

Ownership of the top banks in the EC

It has already been mentioned that a major feature that
distinguishes continental Europe banking systems from British-
type systems is that publicly controlled banks (whether controlled
by central or local government) are much more important in EC
countries outside the United Kingdom.

This is evidenced if we consider the ownership characteristics of
the sample of large banks examined in the previous sector. Table
12.3 shows that out of the top 162 EC banks in 1987, 69 were
privately owned and 67 publicly owned. The mean performance
figures for the public banks are marginally worse than that for
private banks although it could be fair to say that both sectors
exhibit remarkably similar characteristics apart from the average
number of employees. The average public bank employs half as
many staff as the private banks. This is a rather unusual finding, the
reasons for which are not immediately clear, it could be the case
that central management costs and staffing levels of some public
banks are hidden in government accounts.

Credit co-operatives tend to be larger than their public and
private bank counterparts and this is because they are central
institutions representing thousands of small operations. The mutual
institutions are the smallest category and tend to be much smaller in
size even though their return on assets and capital figures are
comparable with the private and public banks. These observations
are also confirmed if we examine the structural and performance
measures for these sectors between 1985 and 1987.

Note that out of the top 162 banks in the EC, 93 are not run for a commercial profit or to satisfy the requirements of private shareholders. These institutions cannot be acquired through hostile takeover. Even though various countries, such as Denmark are currently establishing legislation which will enable mutual societies to convert to corporate status, there will not be many mergers and acquisitions activity between these groups until widespread conversion from public to private ownership takes place.

Table 12.3 *Statistical Summary of the Ownership of Top Banks in the EC, 1987* (all figures arithmetic means)

No. of EC banks in *Banker's* Top 500		Assets $ million	PTP Assets	PTP/ CAP	PTP/ Assets	CAP/ Assets	NINT/	Empl- oyees
Private	69	37601	207.2	0.77	16.36	4.81	3.01	15948
		(1.15)	(1.61)	(0.89)	(0.80)	(0.48)	(0.59)	(1.36)
Public (central & local govt)	67	31133	158.9	0.62	14.30	3.70	2.14	7261
		(1.09)	(1.43)	(1.1)	(0.66)	(0.54)	(0.60)	(1.48)
Cooperative	14	41402	242.8	0.89	17.31	5.16	2.06	12124
		(1.36)	(0.95)	(0.60)	(0.40)	(0.58)	(0.62)	(1.69)
Mutuals	12	10421	77.5	0.81	14.78	6.14	3.99	4419
		(0.50)	(0.64)	(0.46)	(0.52)	(0.39)	(0.29)	(0.56)

Notes: 1. Classification after Revell (1987). Large German savings banks are controlled by local government organisations and therefore are classified as public rather than mutual organisations
2. Figures in parentheses are standard deviations/means
3. PTP – pre-tax profits
   CAP – capital
   NINT – net interest income

Source: Author's estimates from *Banker* '500'

Remember, however, that many public, co-operative and mutual banks operate in the same way as private banks and their ownership status does not preclude them from being aggressive acquirers of private banking institutions. One could be as bold as to state that out of these top 162 banks, 93 cannot be acquired, around 25–27 are too large and nationally too important to let any foreign predator acquire, so that would leave 42–44 medium to large-sized banks that are potential acquisition targets. A geographical breakdown of these banks is given in Table 12.4.

Table 12.4 Potential Big Bank Acquisition Targets in the EC up to 1992

Geographical distribution of top 69 EC private banks	Country	Number of acquisition targets	Name of bank		Asset size ($m) 1987	EC ranking	Majority controlled[1]
3	Belgium	0		—	—	—	
6	Denmark	4	(CB)	Privatbanken	15871	86	
			(CB)	Provinsbanken	9447	116	
			(CB)	Andelsbanken Danebank	7861	128	
			(CB)	Jyske Bank	7601	131	
9	France	5-6	(CB)	Banque Indosuez	47775	36	M
			(CB)	Al-Ubaf Banking Group	14351	92	M
			(FH)	SOVAC	7204	135	M
			(CB)	Eurobank	6373	140	M
			(CB)	Banque Sudameris	5104	157	M
			(CB)	Schlumberger Mallet	5100	158	M
8	Germany	5-6	(CB)	Bayerische Hypotheken und Wechsel Bank	79851	20	
			(CB)	Berliner Handels und Frankfurter Bank	19190	75	M
			(CB)	Westfalenbank	14754	91	
			(CB)	Vereins and Westbank	11649	101	
			(SB)	Industrie Kredit Bank	10612	109	
			(MB)	Sal Oppenheim	7995	127	
1	Greece	0		—	—	—	
2	Ireland	0		—	—	—	
7	Italy	7	(CB)	Banca Nationale dell'Agricoltura	22361	66	M
			(CB)	Banca di Santo Spirito	19793	71	M
			(CB)	Nuovo Banco Ambrosiano	17882	80	M
			(CB)	Credito Romagnolo	11367	104	
			(CB)	Mediobanca	10828	107	M
			(CB)	Banca Cattolica del Veneto	8875	121	

5	Luxembourg	5	(CB)	Banca San Paolo Brescia	5436	149
			(CB)	BCII Holdings	17505	81
			(CB)	Banque Internationale a Luxembourg	11376	103
			(CB)	Banque Generale du Luxembourg	10311	112
			(CB)	Kredietbank Luxembourgeoise	8235	124
			(MB)	BAII Group	5200	156	M
3	Netherlands	0			—	—
1	Portugal	0			—	—
7	Spain	5	(CB)	Banco Hispano Americano	30866	50
			(CB)	Banco Espanol de Credito	30797	51
			(CB)	Banco Popular Espanol	16617	84
			(CB)	Banco de Sabadell	5380	151
15	United Kingdom	11	(CB)	Standard Chartered	55649	32
			(CB)	Royal Bank of Scotland	31159	47
			(CB)	TSB Group	29462	54
			(CB)	Bank of Scotland	19480	73
			(MB)	Kleinwort Benson Group	15025	89
			(MB)	Morgan Grenfell	11102	105
			(DH) (MB)	Gerrard and National Holdings	7808	129
			(CB)	Scandinavia Bank	5858	146
			(MB)	S.G. Warburg	5412	150	M
			(MB)	Hambros	5100	15
			(MB)	Schroders	5091	160

Notes: 1   M denotes that the bank is already majority controlled by another, or group, of institutions

CB   Commercial bank
MB   Merchant bank
SB   Specialist medium and long-term finance bank
FH   Finance house
DH   Discount house

We can see that the country with potentially the largest number of acquisitions targets is the United Kingdom with 11 followed by Italy with 7, and Germany, France, Spain and Luxembourg each with 5 or 6. In addition, around one dozen of the banks in this group are either merchant banks or specialist operators that have little regional significance.

They have very limited branch networks. Thirteen banks out of 44 are already controlled by other institutions or groups of institutions. From this analysis it seems clear that there are only a handful of large banks that can be viewed as potential acquisition targets prior to 1992 and the value of these banks will no doubt demand a distinct market premium over the coming years. If acquisition activity is focused anywhere it will be in the United Kingdom, Germany, Italy, Spain and (possibly) Luxembourg. It seems inevitable that no widespread acquisitions of large banks will take place in the run-up to 1992. By implication, many smaller sized local and regional-based banks may become foreign owned. The limited takeover opportunities available to large banks may encourage them to establish branch networks overseas and there could well be fierce competition and widespread growth in branch numbers where entry via takeover is restricted. Limited takeover opportunities will also accelerate the current move of large banks to form joint ventures with institutions in EC countries.

CONCLUSION

Structural change in EC banking markets will be primarily determined by the ability of the larger EC banks to exploit profitable acquisition opportunities across country boundaries. This chapter shows that out of the top 162 banks in the EC, 93 are not run for a commercial profit or to satisfy the requirements of private shareholders. Around 25 to 27 are probably too large or nationally too important for any home government to let any foreign predator acquire, so that leaves 42–44 large banks that are potential acquisition targets. The majority of these are based in the United Kingdom, Germany, France, Spain, Italy and Luxembourg. If we disregard merchant and specialist banks together with those that are already majority controlled by banks and financial institutions, this leaves us with around 20 to 25 large banks that are potential acquisition targets in the run up to 1992. These limited takeover opportunities available to large banks may encourage them to either establish branch networks, create joint ventures or purchase small to medium sized local and regional banks in other EC countries. Various large EC banks already own small foreign branch networks, like Deutsche Bank with Banca d'America e d'Italia, and these may choose organic growth or small scale acquisitions. Banks that have strong retail as well as small to medium corporate banking aspirations must make acquisitions if they are to make their presence felt. Those, like the Japanese, that are 'currently' intent on doing investment banking business, will establish new or extend limited operations, although they will probably study Table 12.4 with great interest.

References and further reading

Gardener, E.P.M. and Molyneux, P. (1990) *Changes in European Banking* (London: Allen & Unwin).

Molyneux, P. (1989) '1992 and its impact on local and regional banking markets', *Regional Studies*, December.

Revell, J.R.S. (1987) *Mergers and the Role of Large Banks*, IEF Research Monographs in Banking and Finance, no. 2 (Bangor: UCNW)

GLOSSARY OF TERMS

American depositary receipts (ADRs): In order for a non-US company to raise funds in the US market it needs to issue an ADR. An ADR is a negotiable certificate issued by a US bank and each certificate technically represents one or more American depository share (ADS) (see euroequities).

Asset-backed securities: Securities backed by real or financial assets (e.g. mortgage backed securites/bonds). Asset-backed securities are otherwise known as collateralised securities.

Asset management: This can either refer to the managing of an institution's asset side of the balance sheet (e.g. altering the mix of assets to increase returns or minimise risk) or to the function of managing assets on behalf of a customer.

Asset transformation: The ability of financial intermediaries to transform large denomination assets into smaller units.

Automated teller machines (ATMs): An unmanned terminal, usually operated through the use of a magnetically coded card, which can dispense cash, take instructions on transfer, provide balances etc.

Balance of payments: A financial statement prepared for a country which summarises the flow of goods, services and funds between the residents of that country and the residents of the rest of the world during a certain period of time.

Bank for International Settlements (BIS): An international bank set up in Basle in 1930 which has developed into a bank for European central banks and a major source of data on the eurocurrency markets.

Bankers acceptance: A bill of exchange endorsed by a bank. The bank has given its guarantee that payment will be forthcoming from it, not from the buyer. It is a popular way of financing trade transactions.

Base rate: Interest rate used for pricing variable rate loans, e.g. LIBOR.

Bill of exchange: A means of payment used in domestic (rarely) and international banking. Defined by the Bills of Exchange Act of 1882 as 'An unconditional order in writing, addressed by one person to another, signed by the person giving it, requiring the person to whom it is addressed to pay, on demand or at a fixed or determinable future time, a sum certain in money to, or to the order of, a specified person, or to bearer'.

Bond: A document issued by a government or company borrowing money from the public, stating the existence of a debt and the amount owing to the holder of the document (the bondholder). Bondholders use the document to obtain repayment of the loan. Bonds are usually long-term (greater than 5 years maturity) and pay fixed rates of interest.

Broker: An intermediary between the market makers and investors. Brokers buy and sell securities on behalf of customers and do not take a position in securities.

Building society: Financial institution which issues shares (i.e. accepts deposits) and lends to borrowers mainly for home mortgages.

Capital: Generally regarded as shareholders' equity plus subordinated debentures and provisions (see Chapter 11 for a detailed exposition of the BIS capital adequacy proposals).

Capital markets: Markets where capital funds (debt and equity) are issued and traded. This includes private placement sources of debt and equity as well as organised markets and exchanges.

Certificates of deposits (CDs): A negotiable certificate issued by a bank as evidence of an interest-bearing time deposit.

Commercial bank: An institution that carries on traditional banking activities such as deposits taking, granting loans and offering cheque accounts.

Commercial bills: Bills of exchange issued either by a commercial or financial institution.

Commercial credit: Loans and other forms of credit extended to financial and non-financial companies.

Commercial paper: A short-term unsecured promise to repay a fixed amount (representing borrowed funds plus interest) on a certain future date at a specific place. Usually issued by companies with a high credit standing. It may be a purely financial instrument or be based on an underlying commercial transaction.

Commitments: A legal commitment undertaken by a bank to lend to a customer.

Concentration ratio: Measure used to identify the proportion of a total market controlled by the largest firms. In the case of banks, for example, a three-firm concentration ratio measures the proportion of total assets (or total deposits) of the banking sector held by the three largest firms.

Consumer credit: Loans and other forms of credit extended to the household sector. Otherwise known as retail credit.

Convergence: Harmonisation of international standards on bank capital adequacy requirements.

Credit risk: The risk that a counterparty defaults on some or all of its contractual obligations. Credit risk in lending operations is the likelihood that a borrower will not be able to repay the principal or pay the interest.

Cross elasticity of demand: Measure of the degree of responsiveness of the demand for one good to a change in the price of some other goods.

Currency swaps: A transaction in which two counterparties exchange specific amounts of two different currencies at the outset and repay over time according to a predetermined rule which reflects interest payments and possibly amortisation of principal. The payment flows in currency swaps (in which payments are based on fixed interest rates in each currency) are generally like those of spot and forward currency transactions.

Customer information files (CIFs): Information databases containing financial and other characteristics of individual customers. Data is usually used for marketing purposes.

Debentures: Unsecured obligations of an issuing firm, which are claims only on the general assets of the company.

Default: The inability to ultimately fulfil a contractual obligation when it falls due.

Demand deposit: Current account funds that can be withdrawn at any time without notice. They can be either interest or non-interest bearing. Sometimes known as chequeing accounts.

Deposit insurance: Where bank deposits of retail customers are insured against loss in the event of bank failure. Deposit insurance schemes can be privately funded (by the banks) or by the government.

Developing countries: The World Bank classifies these as countries which had an average income per head in 1984 of less than $5000. Sometimes referred to as less developed countries (LDCs).

Discount: A sum of money allowed for immediate payment of a sum due at a later date. If the sum is secured by a bill of exchange, the holder who buys the bill and receives the discount is said to discount the bill.

Disintermediation: The process whereby borrowers and investors by-pass banks and transact business directly.

ECU: European Currency Unit is a composite currency made up of currencies of the members of the European Community (EC).

EFTPOS: Electronic funds transfer at point of sale. A system which allows funds to be transferred automatically as goods are bought in a store.

EFTS: Electronic funds transfer system. A system which transfers funds by means of electronic communication rather than paper.

Equity: In the context of capital markets, equity refers to an ordinary share. In accounting and legal terms, it refers to the financial interests in a firm's assets after prior claims have been made.

Eurobank: Banks and other financial intermediaries that bid for wholesale time deposits and make wholesale loans in a currency or currencies other than that of the country in which they are based.

Eurobond: An international bond that may be issued in any currency and subsequently traded in international markets. Bonds are under-written by syndicates of banks.

Eurocommercial paper: Note sold in London for same-day settlement in US dollars in New York. The maturities are more tailored to the needs of issuers and investors rather than the standard euronote terms of 1, 3 and 6 months.

Eurocurrency: A currency that is held in the form of time deposits in financial institutions outside the home country of the currency, e.g. yen time deposits held in London banks.

Eurodollar: Dollar time deposits held in banks outside the United States. These banks can be foreign owned or overseas branches of US banks.

Euroequities: Equities underwritten and distributed to investors outside the country of origin of the issuer.

Euromarkets: General term that refers to all the markets in which financial instruments denominated in eurocurrencies are traded, e.g. eurobonds, euroequities, etc.

Euronote: A short-term note (usually 1, 3 or 6 months) issued under a note issuance facility (NIF) or eurocommercial paper facility.

European Monetary System: An agreement between various members of the European Community governing exchange market activities. The agreements generally require members to manage closely the exchange values of their currencies relative to other members.

Exchange controls: These are restrictions placed on the movements of funds in a particular currency (or limitations on the convertibility of a currency) imposed by central banking authorities.

Factoring: Raising finance either by selling trade debts or using them as security for borrowing.

Finance houses: Financial institutions which accept deposits and finance leasing and hire purchase agreements.

Financial futures: Futures contracts in an interest rate, stock index, currency or interest bearing security.

Financial Services Act: The Financial Services Act 1986 established the regulatory framework for investor protection in the United Kingdom.

Floating rate debt: Debt instruments that pay a variable (as opposed to fixed) rate of interest.

Floating rate note: A medium term security which carries a floating rate of interest which is reset at regular intervals, usually quarterly or half-yearly, in relation to some predetermined reference rate, typically LIBOR (see LIBOR).

Futures contract: An exchange traded contract generally calling for the delivery of a specified amount of a particular commodity, or financial instrument, at a fixed date in the future.

Gilt-edged securities: UK government bonds.

Globalisation: General term used to describe the worldwide integration of both capital and money markets.

Government bonds: Bonds issued on behalf of (or backed up by) the government.

Guarantees: These are traditional off-balance sheet exposures, where a bank has underwritten the obligations of a third party and currently stands behind the risk, e.g. standby letters of credit and acceptances.

Hedge: To reduce risk by taking a position which offsets existing or expected exposures. Hedging is the avoidance of risk by arranging a contract at specified prices which will yield a known return.

High net worth individuals (HNWIs): Wealthy personal (retail) customers.

HOBS: Home and Office Banking Systems. Banking facilities provided in the home or office through the means of a TV screen, personal computer or telephone.

Household information files: Information databases containing financial files (HIFs) and other characteristics of households. Data is usually used for marketing purposes.

Inspection: Term relating to when bank regulators demand to inspect the books of a bank. Inspection is often undertaken on the banks' own premises.

Inter-bank: Usually refers to short-term loans traded between banks on the parallel money markets.

Interest rate swaps: A transaction in which two counterparties exchange interest payment streams of differing character based on an underlying notional principal amount. The three main types are coupon swaps (fixed rate to floating rate in the same currency), basis swaps (one floating rate index to another floating rate index in the same currency), and cross-currency interest rate swaps (fixed rate in one currency to floating rate in another).

Interest spreads: Difference between interest paid and interest owned, e.g. if interest paid on deposits averages 4 per cent and interest earned on assets equals 10 per cent then the interest spread is 6 per cent.

Intermediary: An intermediary links borrowers and lenders either by acting as an agent, or by bringing together potential traders, or by acting in place of a market.

Internationalisation: General term used to describe the substantial increase in the presence of banks and other financial institutions doing business outside their domestic markets.

Investment bank: An American financial institution that specialises in securities markets activities including underwriting, trading and advisory activities relating to mergers and acquisitions. In the United Kingdom they are known as merchant banks (see merchant bank).

Jobber: A firm, or individual, in the Stock Exchange responsible for quoting prices to and trading securities via brokers.

Leasing: A financial technique for obtaining the use of an asset by contracting a series of payments over a specific period.

Lender of last resort: The understanding that the central bank will always stand ready to lend money to a limited number of financial institutions if they cannot obtain finance from market sources.

Liability management: The process where banks manage liabilities and buy in (i.e. borrow) funds when needed from the markets for interbank deposits, large-sized time deposits and certificates of deposit.

LIBID: London Interbank Bid Rate. The rate at which a bank is willing to buy funds in the international interbank markets.

LIBOR: London Interbank Offered Rate. The rate at which a bank is willing to lend funds (wholesale money) in the international interbank market.

Licensed deposit takers: An institution licensed by the Bank of England under the 1979 Banking Act to take deposits from the public. The 1987 Banking Act abandoned this classification (see recognised banks).

LIMEAN: The mean of LIBID and LIBOR.

Liquid asset: An asset which can easily be turned into cash at short notice.

Liquidity: The ability of an institution to pay its obligations when they fall due.

Liquidity risk: The risk that a solvent institution is temporarily unable to meet its monetary obligations.

Market capitalisation: Market value of a company's outstanding equity.

Market maker: An institution that quotes bid and offer prices for a security and is ready to buy and sell at such prices.

Market segmentation: A systematic process whereby different types of groups are identified (segmented) for target marketing purposes.

Maturity: The length of time elapsing before a debt is to be redeemed by the issuer.

Medium term notes (MTNs): Medium term debt, securities that pay floating rates of interest.

Merchant bank: A UK financial institution that specialises in securities markets activities such as underwriting and trading and advising on such issues as mergers and acquisitions. Merchant banking also refers to acquisition of equity stakes in companies either for strategic or temporary investment purposes. In the United States banks that do this kind of business are referred to as investment banks.

Money market: Short-term financial market usually involving assets with less than one year to maturity.

Mortgage backed bonds: Bonds traded mainly in the United States which pay interest on a semi-annual basis and repay principal either periodically or at maturity, and where the underlying collateral is a pool of mortgages.

Mutual fund: An institution that manages collectively funds obtained from different investors. In the United States they are referred to as mutual funds, in the United Kingdom, unit trusts.

Net interest margin: Gross interest income minus gross interest expense.

Note: A certificate of indebtedness like a bond, but used most frequently for short-term issues.

Note issuance facility (NIF): A medium-term arrangement enabling borrowers to issue short-term paper, typically of three or six months' maturity, in their own names. Usually a group of underwriting banks guarantees the availability of funds to the borrower by purchasing any unsold notes at each rollover date or by providing a standby credit. Facilities produced by competing banks are called, variously, revolving underwriting facilities (RUFs), note purchase facilities and euronote facilities.

Off-balance sheet activities: Banks' business, often fee-based, that does not generally involve booking assets and taking deposits. Examples are swaps, options, foreign exchange futures, standby commitments and letters of credit.

Option: The contractual right, but not the obligation, to buy or sell a specific amount of a given financial instrument at a previously fixed price or a price fixed at a designated future date. A traded option refers to a specific option traded on official markets. A call option confers on the holder the right to buy the financial instrument. A put option involves the right to sell.

Ordinary shares (see equity): Security representing the claim to the residual ownership of a company.

Over-the-counter (OTC) market: An informal dealer-based market.

Own funds directive: EC directive adopted by Council of Ministers in April 1989. The aim is to harmonise the definition of capital for credit institutions.

Preference shares (see equity): Shares which pay a fixed dividend and ranks prior to the ordinary shares in liquidation.

Price elasticity of demand: A measure of the degree of responsiveness of demand to a given change in price.

Primary market: Market in which securities are traded between issuers and investors, thereby raising additional funds for the issuing firm.

Private banking: Specialist banking services provided to very wealthy personal customers, e.g. Swiss bank account facilities.

Prudential regulation: Regulations governing the supervision of the banking system, e.g. licensing criteria, definitions of types of business banks can do, capital adequacy requirements, etc.

Recognised banks: Financial institutions which meet all the requirements set out in the 1979 Banking Act and are recognised as banks by the Bank of England. This classification was abandoned after the 1987 Banking Act (see licenced deposit takers).

Reserve requirement: The proportion of a commercial bank's total assets which it keeps in the form of liquid assets.

Retail banking: Banking services provided to the household (consumer) sector.

Revolving lines of credit: A commitment by a bank to lend to a customer under predefined terms. The commitments generally contain covenants allowing the bank to refuse to lend if there has been a material adverse change in the borrower's financial condition.

Revolving underwriting facilities (RUFs): Similar to a NIF but differs from it because issuers are guaranteed the funds by an underwriting group which buys the notes at a minimum price.

Risk-assets ratio: A ratio that sets out to appraise a bank's capital adequacy on the basis of a bank's relative riskiness.

Savings bank: A financial institution whose primary function is to offer savings facilities to retail customers. It is a mutual institution (like a building society), i.e. it is established and controlled by groups of people for their own benefit.

Secondary market: A market in which previously issued securities are traded.

Securities house: A non-bank organisation that specialises in brokerage and dealing activities in securities.

Securitisation: The term is most often used narrowly to mean the process by which traditional bank or thrift institution assets, mainly loans or mortgages, are converted into negotiable securities which may be purchased either by depository institutions or by non-bank investors. More broadly, the term refers to the development of markets for a variety of new negotiable instruments, such as NIFs and FRNs in the international markets and commercial paper in the United States, which replace bank loans as a means of borrowing. Used in the latter sense, the term often suggests disintermediation of the banking system, as investors and borrowers bypass banks and transact business directly.

Solvency: The ability of an institution to repay obligations ultimately.

Solvency ratio directive: Proposed EC directive aimed to harmonise solvency ratios (capital adequacy ratios) for credit institutions. Common position agreed July 1989. Similar to the BIS convergence proposals discussed in Chapter 8.

Sterling commercial paper: A collective name for short-term unsecured notes issued by corporate borrowers. The majority are issued at maturities between 15 and 45 days.

Stockbrokers: See brokers.

Swap: A financial transaction in which two bodies agree to exchange streams of payment over time according to a predetermined rule. A swap is normally used to transform interest rate or foreign exchange characteristics from one form (i.e. fixed to variable interest) into another (see currency swaps and interest rate swaps).

Third market: UK capital market where listing requirements are less onerous than the Unlisted Securities Market.

Transmutation of claims: Borrowing money on a short-term basis and lending long-term, e.g. building societies provide a striking example of the transmutation function, borrowing short-term in the form of retail deposits and lending to home buyers on as much as a 25 year repayment basis.

Treasury bill: A financial security issued through the discount market by the government as a means of borrowing money for short periods of time (usually three months).

Unit trust: A UK institution that manages collectively funds obtained from different investors (see mutual funds).

Universal bank: An institution which combines its strictly commercial activities with operations in market segments traditionally covered by investment banks and securities houses such as portfolio management, brokerage of securities, underwriting, mergers and acquisitions. A universal bank undertakes the whole range of banking activities.

Unlisted Securities Market: Market for dealing in company stocks and shares that have not obtained a full stock exchange quotation.

Venture capital: Share capital or loans subscribed to a firm by financial specialists when these companies are considered to be high risk and would not normally attract conventional finance.

Wholesale banking: The borrowing and lending of large amounts of money, usually between banks or other financial organisations, through the interbank market.

INDEX